Mark Water

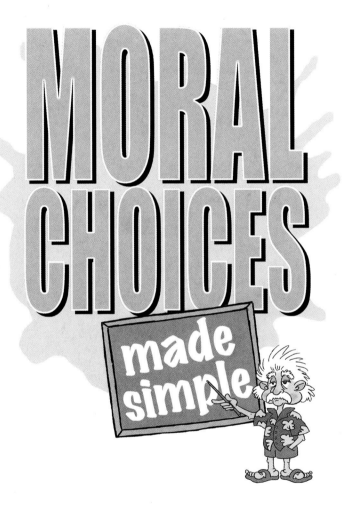

MORAL CHOICES made simple

AMG
Publishers

God's Word is our highest calling.

AMG Publishers
6815 Shallowford Road
Chattanooga, Tennessee 37421

Copyright © 2002 John Hunt Publishing Ltd
Text © 2002 Mark Water

ISBN 0-89957-431-9

Designed by Andrew Milne Design

Printed in China.

Contents

The moral maze

Christians all agree that we should turn to the pages of the Bible when we are in need of encouragement, inspiration and guidance for our spiritual life and walk with God. They also accept that the Bible should be studied when we want to sort out our ideas about the nature of God, life and death.

But it is not so readily accepted that the Bible should be our yardstick and major resource on ethical matters. In fact, many people, including not a few Christians, would never even think of trying to find any help from the Bible on moral issues. After all, they argue, on some issues, such as polygamy and slavery, the teaching of the Bible seems less than clear and, they go on to argue, even runs counter to accepted standards of morality.

On some moral issues (Shouldn't all Christians be pacifists? Should all Christians support capital punishment?), there appears to be no simple answer in the pages of the Bible with the result that Christians are hopelessly divided about what they think.

Then on some issues, such as contemporary medical advances (Should cloning be permitted? Should stem cells from embryos be allowed to be used in a hope for a cure for Alzheimer's disease?), the Bible may appear to be totally irrelevant since such possibilities were never even imagined in Bible times.

This volume, however, sets out principles laid out in the Bible, which, perhaps to many people's surprise, have a direct bearing on even the latest moral dilemmas of the twenty-first century.

Each day we all make moral decisions. Such decisions reveal who we are. Some of our decisions have more to do with selfishness than following God's will. Who does not find it easier to make decisions in favor of personal freedom when the alternative is one of tough responsibility?

THE DECLINE OF MORAL STANDARDS		
Ideology	*Time*	*Belief*
Biblical morality	1800–1900s	There is such a thing as right and wrong. Certain things are right and wrong, and I know why.
Abiblical morality	1900–1950s	Certain things are right and wrong, but I don't know why.
Immorality	1960–early 1970s	Certain things are right and wrong, but I don't care.
Amorality	Late 1970–present	There is no such thing as right or wrong!

Moral decline

In our society at large it is possible to trace a worldwide movement away from what used to be recognized as wholesome moral standards.

It is in the face of the table on the opposite page, which is only meant to be a rough and ready list of generalizations charting a trend in moral attitudes, that Christians should not lose their nerve but find out what the unchanging biblical standards are and apply them to our ever-changing, and increasingly complex moral problems.

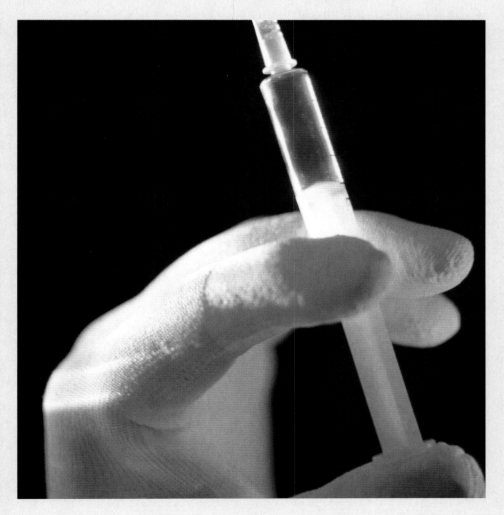

1 BIBLE PRINCIPLES

Introduction

Paul

When Paul wrote to the Corinthians he did not tone down his moral teaching to make it more palatable to Christians living in an immoral society. Today it is always a fatal mistake to attempt to tailor biblical teaching to the mood of the day.

Culturally dated, but permanently valid

When looking to the Bible for guidance on moral questions to do with the society in which God has placed us we have to be aware of what is permanently valid and what is culturally dated.

As we interpret the Bible we do not close our eyes to the particular situation, historical moment and geographical location in which it was originally given. The more we know about the social customs of the Old and New Testaments the better.

But just because we can point to many instances in the Bible which show that it is culturally dated does not give us

liberty to reject its teaching. On the other hand, we are not meant to elevate biblical cultural behavior to the status of permanent validity.

Rather we should accept that the *teaching* of the Bible is permanently valid. At the same time we should translate its cultural setting into our own contemporary cultural terms.

Foot-washing

For example, in John 13:12-17, Jesus ordered his disciples to wash one another's feet. "You should do as I have done for you" John 13:15. This was to be done as a mark of mutual love, which is quite happy to humble itself in the service of others. That is the principle that remains forever valid.

But it does not mean that we are to wash the feet of all Christians we meet. For in the West we no longer walk through hot and dust-filled streets. So foot-washing is not needed. But the need for humble service never ends.

What are the Bible principles that apply to all moral problems?

The Christian's checklists about moral questions

About any course of action or moral dilemma we can ask the following four questions:

1. What are the overriding considerations?
2. How will it affect others?
3. How will it affect my relationship to God?
4. How will it affect me?

	Questions to ask	Scriptures to apply
	CHECKLIST A: OVERRIDING CONSIDERATIONS	
1.	Will it bring glory to God?	So whether you eat or drink or whatever you do, do it all for the glory of God. 1 Corinthians 10:31
2.	Will this give the devil an opportunity?	Do not give the devil a foothold. *Ephesians 4:27*
3.	Is there anything in the Bible contrary to it?	To the law and to the testimony. If they [godless people] do not speak according to this word, they have no light of dawn. *Isaiah 8:20*
4.	Is it evil?	Avoid every kind of evil. *1 Thessalonians 5:22*
5.	Is it right or wrong in itself?	All wrongdoing is sin. 1 John 5:17
6.	Can I do this in Jesus' name?	And whatever you do, whether in word or deed, do it all in the name of the Lord Jesus, giving thanks to God the Father through him. *Colossians 3:17*
7.	Do I know in my heart that it's sinful?	If I had cherished sin in my heart, the Lord would not have listened. *Psalm 66:18*
8.	Can I pray about it?	…in everything, by prayer and petition… *Philippians 4:6*
9.	What would my pastor think about it?	Remember your leaders, who spoke the word of God to you. Consider the outcome of their way of life and imitate their faith. *Hebrews 13:7*
10.	Would I like to be doing this when Jesus Christ returns?	And now, dear children, continue in him, so that when he appears we may be confident and unashamed before him at his coming. *1 John 2:27*
11.	How will it affect the world, and all who live in it?	The earth is the Lord's, and everything in it. *Psalm 24:1*

CHECKLIST B: HOW WILL IT AFFECT OTHERS?	
Questions to ask	*Scriptures to apply*
1. Will it make somebody else fall?	It is better not to eat meat or drink wine or do anything else that will cause your brother to fall. *Romans 14:21*
2. Will it build up someone else's faith?	All of these must be done for the strengthening of the church. *1 Corinthians 14:26*
3. Some things do not edify others.	"Everything is permissible" – but not everything is beneficial. *1 Corinthians 10:23*
4. What about a person with a weak conscience?	For if anyone with a weak conscience sees you who have this knowledge eating in an idol's temple, won't he be emboldened to eat what has been sacrificed to idols? *[ref?]*

CHECKLIST C: HOW WILL IT AFFECT MY RELATIONSHIP TO GOD?	
Questions to ask	*Scriptures to apply*
1. Will this cause me to be tempted?	Do not think about how to gratify the desires of the sinful nature. *Romans 13:14*
2. Am I trusting God or my own strength?	Trust in the Lord with all your heart and lean not on your own understanding. *Proverbs 3:5*
3. Would the Lord Jesus Christ do this?	To this you were called, because Christ suffered for you, leaving you an example, that you should follow in his steps. *1 Peter 2:22*
4. Is it putting Jesus first?	...for I always do what pleases him. *John 8:29*
5. Will it help to make Jesus supreme?	He [Christ] is the head of body, the church... so that in everything he might have the supremacy. *Colossians 1:18*
6. Will it defile God's body?	Do you not know that your body is a temple of the Holy Spirit, who is in you, whom you have received from God? *1 Corinthians 6:19*

MORAL CHOICES MADE SIMPLE | 11

WHAT ARE THE BIBLE PRINCIPLES THAT APPLY TO ALL MORAL PROBLEMS?

Knowing God's will and pleasing the Lord

Paul is certain that it is possible that we can know God's will and that we can grow in knowledge of God's will. This is the way to really please God, says Paul

"For the reason, since the day we heard about you, we have not stopped praying for you and asking God to fill you with *the knowledge of his will* through all spiritual wisdom and understanding. And we pray this in order that you may live a life worthy of the Lord and may please him in every way: bearing fruit in every good work, *growing in the knowledge of God."*
Colossians 1:9-10

Are Christians above reproach?

Well, we reply, we certainly should be.

CHECKLIST D: HOW WILL IT AFFECT ME?	
Questions to ask	*Scriptures to apply*
1. Am I in two minds about doing this?	But the man who has doubts is condemned if he eats, because his eating is not from faith; and everything that does not come from faith is sin. *Romans 14:23*
2. Am I doing it out of selfishness?	Do nothing out of selfish ambition or vain conceit. *Philippians 2:2*
3. Am I showing off about my own spirituality?	Now a man named Ananias, together with his wife Sapphira, also sold a piece of property. With his wife's full knowledge he kept back part of the money for himself. *Acts 5:1-2*
4. Am I denying myself?	If anyone would come after me, he must deny himself... *Luke 9:23*
5. Am I deceiving myself?	Do not deceive yourselves. If any one of you thinks he is wise by the standards of this age, he should become a "fool" so that he may become wise. *1 Corinthians 3:18*
6. Am I justifying my action in the sight of men?	You are the ones who justify yourselves in the eyes of men, but God knows your hearts. What is highly valued among men is detestable in God's sight. *Luke 16:15*

But we know that this is all too often just not the case.

A survey conducted by the Roper Organization found that behavior deteriorated after "born again" experiences.

Drink

While only 4% of respondents said they had driven intoxicated before being "born again," 12% had done so after conversion.

Drugs

Similarly, 5% had used illegal drugs before conversion, 9% after.

Sex

2% admitted to engaging in illicit sex before salvation; 5% after.

How much we need morality

Most people agree that every society needs some kind of morality to live by. But if we were to go by the morality communicated by many of the tabloid

MORAL CHOICES MADE SIMPLE 13

WHAT ARE THE BIBLE PRINCIPLES THAT APPLY TO ALL MORAL PROBLEMS?

newspapers and many of the TVv soaps we would end up by living by the law of the jungle.

There are many moralities around and it is of vital importance that we choose the "right" one.

Amoral morality

1. Morality according to Auguste Comte:
   "All is relative."

2. Morality according to Jean-Paul Satre:
   "If God exists man cannot be free. But man is free, therefore God cannot exist.
   Since God does not exist all things are morally permissible."

HOW MUCH WE NEED A CHRISTIAN MORALITY

"IMPROPER" MORALITY
"But among you there must not be even a hint of sexual immorality, or of any kind of impurity, or of greed, because these are improper for God's holy people."
Ephesians 5:3

THE RIGHT WAY
"Better, though difficult, the right way to go
   Than wrong, tho' easy, where the end is woe."
John Bunyan

JESUS' TEACHING
"How is it that nobody has dreamed up any moral advances since Christ's teaching?" *Michael Green*

AN IMMORAL ACT
"Give up money, give up fame, give up science, give up the earth itself and all it contains, rather than do an immoral act."
Thomas Jefferson

A WORLD WITH NO SENSE OF GOOD AND BAD
"If no set of moral ideas were truer or better than any other, there would be no sense in preferring civilized morality to savage morality, or Christian morality to Nazi morality.

The moment you say that one set of moral ideas can be better than another, you are, in fact, measuring them both by a standard, saying that one of them conforms to that standard more nearly than the other."
C. S. Lewis

A MORAL FAITH
"Lord, give us faith that right makes might." *Abraham Lincoln*

A MINORITY OF ONE
"Right is right, even if everyone is against it; and wrong is wrong, even if everyone is for it."
William Penn

There is a war on

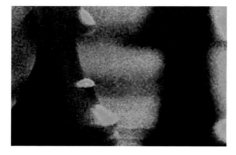

A spiritual battle

Paul likened the Christian life to a spiritual battle: Ephesians 6:10-18. As we consider many of the moral problems that surround us it would be unwise to forget the battle that rages within us.

One of the most neglected parts of the teaching of the Bible concerns the moral battle that rages inside every Christian. To deny it is to be dishonest and to be untrue to the teaching of the Bible. While Christians are forgiven sinners they can still identify with Paul when he says:

> "For what I want to do I do not do, but what I hate I do…
> For I have the desire to do what is good, but I cannot carry it out.
> For what I do is not the good I want to do;
> no, the evil I do not want to do – this I keep on doing."
> *Romans 7:15-19*

Depraved human nature

VERY FAR GONE!
"Man is very far gone from original righteousness."
Book of Common Prayer

TOTAL DEPRAVITY
"Our nature is not only completely empty of goodness, but so full of every kind of wrong that it is always active."
John Calvin

EICHMANN
"Eichmann is in us, each of us."
Dinur

OUR EVIL SPIRIT
"It is easier to denature plutonium that to denature the evil spirit of man."
Albert Einstein

COOKING A GOOD OMELETTE
"No clever arrangement of bad eggs will make a good omelette."
C. S. Lewis

A MONSTER OF DEPRAVITY
"If I wrote down every thought I have ever thought and every deed I have ever done, men would call me a monster of depravity."
Somerset Maugham

Understanding human nature

If we want to help other people we need to know the true nature of human nature.

If we want to become holy we also need to know what the Bible teaches about our human nature.

According to Paul, the acts of our human nature are obvious:

- Worldliness is an act of our human nature, 1 Corinthians 3:3
- Sexual immorality is an act of our human nature
- Impurity is an act of our human nature
- Debauchery is an act of our human nature
- Idolatry is an act of our human nature
- Witchcraft is an act of our human nature
- Hatred is an act of our human nature
- Discord is an act of our human nature
- Jealousy is an act of our human nature
- Fits of rage are an act of our human nature
- Selfish ambition is an act of our human nature
- Dissensions are an act of our human nature
- Factions are an act of our human nature
- Envy is an act of our human nature
- Drunkenness is an act of our human nature
- Orgies are an act of our human nature. See Galatians 5:19-21.

The seven deadly sins

The seven deadly sins, all of which are found in the Bible, also show us what our human nature is like:

ANGER

"But I tell you that anyone who is angry with his brother will be subject to judgment." Matthew 5:22

"Be not angry, for anger leads to murder. Be not jealous or contentious or full of wrath, for of all these things murders are engendered."
Didache

COVETOUSNESS

"Watch out! Be on your guard against all kinds of greed; a man's life does not consist in the abundance of his possessions." Luke 12:15

"The soul of the covetous is far removed from God, as far as the memory, understanding and will are concerned. He forgets God as though God were not his God, owing to the fact that he has fashioned himself a god of Mammon and of temporal possessions."
John of the Cross

ENVY

"Love is patient, love is kind. It does not envy." 1 Corinthians 13:4

"Envy is the diabolical sin."
Augustine

GLUTTONY

"Their god is their stomach."
Philippians 3:19

"Gluttony kills more than the sword" Sixteenth-century proverb

LUST

"They are well-fed, lusty stallions, each neighing for another man's wife." Jeremiah 5:8

"Surely," we say, "such as verse as this must apply to ungodly, unregenerate people?" But no. Jeremiah 5:1 gives us the context, which is God's people, living in God's holy city: "God up and down the streets of Jerusalem." All the Christian moral principles in a book like this should be applied to us as individuals, and to Christian fellowships, before we dare to point any accusing fingers elsewhere. Consider the horrors of child abuse, and the cover up of such rank evil, that have been committed by cardinals, Christian ministers and Christian leaders.

PRIDE

"Pride goes before destruction, a haughty spirit before a fall." Proverbs 16:18

"He was like a rooster who thought the sun had risen to hear him crow." *George Eliot*

SLOTH

The book of Proverbs warns us against sloth many times: Proverbs 10:5; 13:4; 18:9; 19:15.

"Go to the ant, you sluggard; consider its ways and be wise!

It has no commander, no overseer or ruler,

yet it stores its provisions in summer and gathers its food at harvest.

How long will you lie there, you sluggard? When will you get up from your sleep?" *Proverbs 6:6-9*

"If a man is lazy, the rafters sag; if his hands are idle, the house leaks." *Ecclesiastes 10:19*

The antidote

We may be more familiar with the verses about living by the Spirit, the fruit of the Spirit and keeping in step with the Spirit: Galatians 5:16-18, 22-25. But we should not ignore the verses in between.

John Newton

John Newton once said: "I am not what I ought to be; I am not what I want to be; but I am what I am by the grace of God."

Knowing what is right, pointing others in that direction, and doing what is right ourselves, requires constant growth in our own sanctification.

Jesus' basic ethical teaching

The Old Testament and the New Testament

The ethical teaching found in the New Testament is based on the ethical teaching in the Old Testament. And when we come to the teaching of Jesus, there is no suggestion that he started from scratch.

For example, Jesus summed up the Ten Commandments with the dual requirement that we should love God and love our neighbor: Matthew 22:37-39; Mark 12:30; Luke 10:27.

For Jesus, his ethical teaching, as with all the rest of his teaching, was based on two things:

- the Old Testament
- Jesus' recognition of his own personal authority.

Jesus and goodness

Jesus' ethical teaching was based on his knowledge of what was and is good.

Character and motives

When Jesus assessed a person's character he did so by judging his inner motives. Jesus had endless clashes with the scribes and Pharisees because of the emphasis they put on meticulous attention to external acts while neglecting the inner condition. Jesus likened them to sepulchers which looked quite beautiful from the outside, but inwardly were full of rotting corpses, Matthew 23:27-28.

"You are like whitewashed tombs" Matthew 23:27.

The moral law

Mere observance of ceremonial law was never commended by Jesus. Rather, he was concerned about weightier matters of the moral law; with things such as:

- justice
- mercy
- faith, Matthew 23:23.

Jesus based his teaching on the inner character of goodness, rather than legislating on everything under the sun, and giving endless laws to obey. So when Peter asked Jesus how many times he should forgive his brother, Jesus said that he should not stop forgiving his brother before 490 times. In this way Jesus emphasized the importance of having the right moral attitude to a thing, rather than keeping some law, Matthew 18:22; Luke 17:3-4.

So, to obey Jesus meant much more than observing a set of laws, rules and codes; rather it meant to be devoted to the person of Jesus.

Jesus and covetousness

One result of Jesus' view about goodness was that he was outspoken in his condemnation of certain undesirable qualities. Anything that ran counter to the character of true goodness was in line for direct condemnation from Jesus.

Take the example of covetousness. Jesus condemned covetousness, just as the Old Testament did. Jesus told the parable of Dives and Lazarus as a commentary on the evil of covetousness.

For the charge against Dives was not that he possessed wealth, but that he refused to use his wealth to help the poorest people on his doorstep, Luke 16:19-31. Dives' possessions had blinded him to people in need and so his social conscience and concern were destroyed.

Jesus and self-centeredness
In Jesus' ethical teaching he always went to the heart of the matter. He knew that self-centeredness was the root from which so many other evils sprang: evils such as:

- arrogance
- greed
- immorality
- envy
- lack of self-control.

Jesus said quite bluntly that those who keep life for themselves lose it, Luke 17:33.

Jesus taught that self-love was the great stumbling block in personal ethics. So Jesus told his followers that they had to deny themselves if they were truly to be his disciples, Matthew 16:24.

What Jesus condemned
Jesus did not hesitate to condemn sins of the flesh. But Jesus did not just focus on the outward act of fornication, but explained that the desire to fornicate was against God's laws, Matthew 5:28.

In the same way Jesus never condoned the woman caught in the act of adultery.

But he made sure that her accusers realized their own sinfulness, John 8:2-11.

Jesus also condemned anyone who made another person sin, and said that one should go to extreme lengths to ensure that this never happened, Mark 9:43-48.

How are Bible principles to be applied by us today?

Question:
How can a 2,000-year-old book help us with our ethical dilemmas in the twenty-first century?
Answer:
It is because God does not change: Malachi 3:6. He is the same yesterday, today and forever: Hebrews 13:8. God's Word does not change either.

Question:
Ah, but the Bible was written in a different culture, in a pre-industrial age. So how can it apply to us today?
Answer:
Principles like right and wrong, goodness and evil do not change from one generation to another. Such principles remain and can be applied to us and to your great-grandchildren.

Have you ever wondered why Paul should say to Timothy that the Old Testament could equip him for every good work? See 2 Timothy 3:16, 17.

Question:
But won't this mean that we take things out of context, if we use such an ancient volume to guide us?
Answer:
Yes, we have to watch out that in our interpretation of the Bible we do not mistake changing cultural habits for non-changing principles.

We need to be alert. First of all we have to identify the immediate cultural context and the immediate historical context.

But that's not all. Second, we have to see how the text applies to us today: Acts 28:25-27.

Hermeneutics, understanding how the text applies to us, goes hand in hand with exegesis, appreciating what the text meant to its first readers. This is not just true of the Bible; it applies to every ancient writing.

Question:
But if you do this, you'll come up with things that the original author never imagined in his wildest dreams!
Answer:
Yes, we may well. In some senses the

God in the society God has placed us in. To say that we know God, 1 John 2:4, and love God, John 14:15, means precisely this. We are to use our God-given minds, Matthew 22:37, to work out how we should behave today, basing all this on God's principles laid down in his Word.

Question:
But you must surely agree that there are many other contemporary debates that the Bible is silent about.
Answer:
This is just not the case. In fact the Bible has specific teaching about things like theft, murder, and adultery. The problem here is less to do with the Bible and more to do with the euphemistic names given to these evils. For example:

- What the world calls ethnic cleansing the Bible calls murder: Exodus 21:14.
- What the world calls divorce and remarriage the Bible calls adultery: Mark 10:11.
- What the world calls tax evasion the Bible calls theft: Matthew 22:2
- What the world calls insincerity the Bible calls telling lies: Proverbs 26:24.

Belief and behavior

Bible is unlike any other ancient document, but Christians believe that God is its author: 2 Timothy 3:16. So it's our job to see how God's unchanging principles do impact on our present day's problems. This is the case whether or not the original authors of the Bible were aware of this.

Question:
Isn't doing that kind of thing rather beyond your reach?
Answer:
Not really. But it is often far from easy. However it is vitally important. For as Christians we believe that we must obey

"Good conduct arises out of good doctrine." *John Stott*

Some dos and don'ts: don'ts

Negatively

There are many prohibitions in the Bible. But they do not come from a grumpy kill-joy, but are from the loving heart of our heavenly Father. He created us and has given us many guidelines to live by.

- Do not parade your spirituality before people, Matthew 6:1.
- Do not be like the hypocrites, Matthew 6:8.
- Do not judge other people, Matthew 7:1; James 5:9.
- Do not be afraid or troubled, John 6:20; 14:27.
- Do not be faithless but believing, John 20:27.
- Do not be afraid to speak up for Jesus, Acts 18:9.
- Do not let the world squeeze you into its mold, Romans 12:2.
- Do not be lacking in zeal, Romans 12:11.
- Do not be proud, Romans 12:16.
- Do not be conceited, Romans 12:16.
- Do not be divisive, 1 Corinthians 1:10.
- Do not take a fellow-Christian to court, 1 Corinthians 6:1-8.
- Do not be idolatrous, 1 Corinthians 10:7, 14.
- Do not keep company with demons, 1 Corinthians 10:21.
- Do not be yoked with unbelievers, 2 Corinthians 6:14.
- Do not let yourselves be burdened again by a yoke of slavery, Galatians 5:1.

- Do not destroy a fellow-Christians with your "biting and devouring," Galatians 5:15.
- Do not be deceived, Galatians 6:7.
- Do not become fed up with doing good, Galatians 6:9.
- Do not let your angry lead you into sin, Ephesians 4:26.
- Do not be deceived by empty words, Ephesians 5:6.
- Do not be foolish, Ephesians 5:17.
- Do not be ashamed to live for Jesus, Philippians 1:20.
- Do not let go of hope, Colossians 1:23.
- Do not be overcome by trials, 1 Thessalonians 3:3.
- Do not be ignorant about Jesus' return, 1 Thessalonians 4:13.
- Do not be easily alarmed by some spurious prophecy, 2 Thessalonians 2:2.
- Do not be ashamed to witness for Jesus, 2 Timothy 1:8, Matthew 10:32.
- Do not be ashamed to work for God, 2 Timothy 2:15.
- Do not be unfruitful, Titus 3:14.
- Do not make light of God's discipline, Hebrews 12:5:
  "And you have forgotten that word of encouragement that addresses you as sons: 'My son, do not make light of the Lord's discipline, and do not lose heart when he rebukes you, because the Lord disciplines those he loves, and he punishes everyone he accepts as a son.'" Hebrews 12:5-6

- Do not become lazy, Hebrews 6:12.
- Do not forget to entertain strangers, Hebrews 13:2.
- Do not be covetous, Hebrews 13:5.
- Do not be carried away with all kinds of strange teachings, *Hebrews 13:9.*

Negatives can be very positive

The Ten Commandments are cast in a negative form so that we are helped to keep on the straight and narrow. Here are ten tests to see if we have broken God's laws. If we are deliberately breaking God's clear commands, there is little point in trying to discover the right course of action about things we are uncertain about.

1. To love selfish pleasures more than God breaks the first commandment.
2. Religious adoration for man-made objects breaks the second commandment.
3. Flippant and hypocritical use of God's name breaks the third commandment.
4. Not worshiping God in spirit and truth breaks the fourth commandment.
5. Disrespect and disobedience to parents breaks the fifth commandment.
6. Anger and malicious thoughts breaks the sixth commandment.
7. Lustful thoughts and cravings breaks the seventh commandment.
8. Cheating and taking things, including reputations, which rightly belong to other people breaks the eighth commandment.
9. Slanderous statements and gossip breaks the ninth commandment:
   "Let him who takes pleasure in mauling the lives of the absent know that his own is not such as to fit him to sit at this table." *Augustine had this notice displayed at his dinner table.*
10. Coveting what another person has breaks the tenth commandment.

"The soul of the covetous is far removed from God. He forgets God owing to the fact that he has fashioned for himself a god of temporal posessions." *John of the Cross*

Some dos and don'ts: dos

Positively

Many, but not necessarily all, of the moral and ethical questions which face Christians would be alleviated greatly if we managed to live the kind of lives that we are instructed to live in the pages of Scripture.

- Be glad, even under persecution, Matthew 5:12.
- Be perfect, Matthew 5:48.
- Be in a spirit of prayer, Matthew 7:7-8; Romans 12:12.
- Be wise as serpents, Matthew 10:16.
- Be ready to meet Jesus at his second coming, Luke 12:40.
- Be ready for service, Luke 17:8; Romans 12:11.
- Be of good cheer (take heart), John 16:33.
- Be prepared to suffer for Jesus, Acts 21:13.
- Be strong in the faith, Romans 4:20.
- Be dead to self and to sin, Romans 6:11.
- Be alive to God, Romans 6:11.
- Be concerned for those who do not know Jesus, Romans 10:1.
- Be transformed in your thinking, Romans 12:2.
- Be devoted to fellow-Christians in brotherly and sisterly love, Romans 12:10.
- Be full of zeal for Jesus, Romans 12:11.
- Be joyful in hope, Romans 12:12.
- Be patient in affliction, Romans 12:12.

- Be faithful in prayer, Romans 12:12.
- Be generous to those in need, Romans 12:13.
- Be hospitable, Romans 12:13.
- Be sure to live in harmony with fellow-Christians, Romans 12:16.
- Be those who overcome evil with good, Romans 12:21.
- Be afraid to do wrong, Romans 13:4.
- Be faithful, 1 Corinthians 4:2.
- Be awake, 1 Corinthians 15:31.
- Be steadfast, 1 Corinthians 15:58.
- Be reconciled to God, 2 Corinthians 5:20.
- Be separate from ungodliness, 2 Corinthians 6:17.
- Be of good comfort, 2 Corinthians 13:11.
- Be led by God's Holy Spirit,

Galatians 5:18.
- Be considerate, Galatians 6:1.
- Be able to assimilate Jesus' love,
  Ephesians 3:18-19.
- Be renewed in the Spirit,
  Ephesians 4:32.
- Be tenderhearted, Ephesians 4:32.
- Be forgiving, Ephesians 4:32.
- Be followers of God, Ephesians 5:1.
- Be open to understanding God's will,
  Ephesians 5:17.
- Be filled with the Spirit,
  Ephesians 5:18.
- Be strong in the Lord,
  Ephesians 6:10.
- Be able to withstand Satan's attacks,
  Ephesians 6:16.
- Be confident that God's good work
  in you will be carried on until it is
  completed, Philippians 1:6.
- Be sincere, Philippians 1:6.
- Be filled with the fruits of
  righteousness, Philippians 1:11.
- Behave in a way that is worthy of the
  gospel of Christ, Philippians 1:27.
- Be of one mind with Jesus,
  Philippians 2:5.
- Be blameless, Philippians 2:15.
- Be pure, Philippians 2:15.
- Behave as God's children in this
  wicked world, Philippians 2:15.
- Be found in Jesus, Philippians 3:9.
- Be gentle to everyone,
  Philippians 4:5.
- Be anxious about nothing,
  Philippians 4:6.
- Be full of God's peace,
  Philippians 4:7.

- Be content, Philippians 4:11-12.
- Be encouraged in heart,
  Colossians 2:2.
- Be united in love, Colossians 2:2.
- Be truthful, Colossians 3:9.
- Be thankful, Colossians 3:15.
- Be always in full of grace, in your
  conversation, Colossians 4:6.
- Be energetic, 1 Thessalonians 4:11.
- Be full of the glory of Jesus,
  2 Thessalonians 1:12.
- Be an example, 1 Timothy 4:12.
- Be not ashamed to testify about
  Jesus, 2 Timothy 1:8.
- Be not ashamed of fellow-Christians,
  2 Timothy 1:8.
- Be strong in the grace of Jesus,
  2 Timothy 2:1.
- Be kind to everyone,
  2 Timothy 2:24.
- Be able to teach, 2 Timothy 2:24.
- Be thoroughly equipped for every
  good work, by the Scriptures,
  2 Timothy 3:17.
- Be prepared in season and out of
  season, 2 Timothy 4:2.
- Be ready to work, Titus 3:1.
- Be free from the love of money,
  Hebrews 13:5.
- Be content with what you have,
  Hebrews 13:5.
- Be quick to listen, James 1:19.
- Be slow to speak, James 1:19.
- Be slow to become angry,
  James 1:19.
- Be doers of God's Word, James 1:22.
- Be patient about Jesus' return,
  James 5:7-8.

2 *PERSONAL RELATIONSHIPS*

Introduction

How the Bible answers today's questions

The Bible claims to give us all the guidance we need in order to live the Christian life. Peter put it like this: "His divine power has given us everything we need for life and godliness through our knowledge of him who called us by his own glory and goodness." *2 Peter 1:3*

2 Timothy 3:16-17 states that scripture is useful for:

- teaching
- rebuking
- correcting
- training in righteousness.

Christians believe that the Bible gives us all the principles we need to make the correct moral choices in the twenty-first century.

Going with the crowd

Most of us would prefer not to have to stand out in a crowd. Rather, we all too often find it much easier to follow the crowd. This goes for moral decisions. But Bible truth is not determined by majority rule. Exodus 23:2 puts it in a nutshell: "Do not follow the crowd in doing wrong."

- The crowd can be, and often is, wrong.
- The majority of Germans gave their tacit support to Adolph Hitler.
- The majority of Americans at one time supported segregation and the "separate but equal" concept among the races.
- The majority in three crowds in Jerusalem yelled for the deaths of Jesus, Stephen and Paul.

Marriage and divorce

Genesis and marriage

There are three reasons given in the opening chapters of Genesis for marriage.

1. Marriage is for procreation

"Be fruitful and multiply." *Genesis 1:28*

2. Marriage is for companionship

"It is not good for the man to be alone. I will make a helper suitable for him." *Genesis 2:18*

3. Marriage is for self-giving love

"They will become one flesh." *Genesis 2:24*

This self-giving love within a marriage relationship finds its natural expression in sexual union.

Defining marriage

The best definition of marriage in the Bible comes in Genesis 2:24: "For this reason a man will leave his father and mother and be united to his wife, and they will be one flesh."

Marriage exists in God's sight when a man leaves his parents in order to be united to his wife and become one flesh with her.

Genesis 1:14-25

"From Genesis 1:14-25 we learn the following biblical principles about marriage:

- *a man* (as 'man' is in the singular this shows that marriage is an exclusive union between two individuals)
- *shall leave his father and mother* (which seems to indicate a definite break and some public social occasion)
- *and cleave to his wife* (this shows that marriage is a loving and 'cleaving' commitment, which is heterosexual and permanent)

- *and they shall become one flesh*
  (sexual intercourse consummates a
  marriage)

'One flesh' (from these verses we
conclude that the only 'one flesh'
experience which God intends and
Scripture contemplates is sexual
union of a man with his wife, whom
he recognizes as 'flesh of his flesh'."
John Stott

Marriage is...

From the above we see that marriage is:

- an exclusive
- heterosexual
- agreement, that is covenant
- between one man and one woman
- ordained and sealed by God
- preceded by a public leaving of
  parents
- consummated in sexual union,
- which is most often blessed with the
  gift of children.

Question:

Is there anyone I should not marry?

Answer:

Yes. First of all you are not allowed to
marry anyone whom you are closely
related to: Leviticus 18:6-18. This was
Amnon's terrible mistake, see 2 Samuel 13.

Second, you shouldn't even consider
marrying anyone who is already married,
Deuteronomy 22:22, or who is engaged
to be married, Deuteronomy 22:23-24.
This is where David went so wrong.

Question:

But what if I'm in love with a married or
engaged person?

Answer:

Here there are no easy options. Drastic
action is called for. If we do fall in love
with anyone in these categories, we may
become so overwhelmed by our
emotions that all we want to do is to act
on them. That will lead to disaster.
What we should do is to realize that we
are being tempted. And then resist the
temptation, 1 Peter 5:8-9.

Question:

Is it true that Christians should only
marry Christians? What should I do if
I'm in love with a non-Christian?

Answer:

Christians are meant to be God's holy
people, 1 Peter 2:9. We are not meant to
be tied up with unbelievers, 2
Corinthians 6:14-18. So Christians have
concluded that marriages between
Christians and non-Christians are out.
So a Christian should not marry a
person of another faith or anyone who
does not have faith in Jesus.

This teaching comes in the Old
Testament as well as in the New
Testament, Deuteronomy 7:1-6. Some
people in the Old Testament, such as
Solomon, 1 Kings 11:1-2; Ahab, 1 Kings
16:31; and the people of Israel, Ezekiel
9:1-4; 10:1-4; Nehemiah 10:30;
13:23-27, stand as warnings for us to
heed. They were not to marry non-
Israelites.

Is a marriage indissoluble?

Divorce is a dissolution of the marriage bond. Any dissolution of a marriage moves away from God's intention and his ideal in all marriages. Marriages are meant to be lifelong unions.

Divorce breaks the covenant and is seen as an act of treachery, which God hates.

"Another thing you do: You flood the LORD's altar with tears. You weep and wail because he no longer pays attention to your offerings or accepts them with pleasure from your hands. You ask, 'Why?' It is because the LORD is acting as the witness between you and the wife of your youth, because have *broken faith with her*, though she is your partner, the wife of your *marriage covenant*.

Has not the LORD made them one? In flesh and spirit they are his. And why one? Because he was seeking godly offspring. So guard yourself in your spirit, and *do not break faith* with the wife of your youth.

'I hate divorce,' says the LORD God…"
Malachi 2:13-16

Old Testament grounds for divorce

The Old Testament makes provision for divorce but is against divorce. There is only one Old Testament passage that mentions grounds for divorce.

"If a man marries a woman who becomes displeasing to him because he finds something indecent about her, and he writes her a certificate of divorce, gives it to her and sends her from his house, and if after she leaves his house she becomes the wife of another man, and her second husband dislikes her and writes her a certificate of divorce, gives it to her and sends her from his house, or if he dies, then her first husband, who divorced her, is not allowed to marry her again after she has been defiled. That would be detestable in the eyes of the LORD. Do not bring sin upon the land the LORD your God is giving you as an inheritance."
Deuteronomy 24:1-4

What is Deuteronomy 24:1-4 saying?

The main point of these verses is not to do with divorce, or even with certificates of divorce. It is to do with forbidding a man to remarry his former wife, if he had divorced her. For this "would be detestable in the eyes of the LORD," Deuteronomy 24:4. This gave her protection against a former husband who might have been cruel.

These verses are not approving of divorce. All they are saying is that:

- *if* a man divorces his wife,
- *if* he gives a certificate of divorce,
- *if* she leaves and remarries, and
- *if* her second husband dislikes and divorces her, or dies,
- *then* her first husband may not marry her.

Grounds for divorce

These verses are not encouraging divorce. But if a divorce does happen, what then? Here are the grounds for a divorce. They are if a husband "finds something indecent about her," or "something shameful" *NEB, RSV* in his wife.

This does not refer to adultery, as that was then punishable by death, not by divorce, Deuteronomy 22.20-22, compare with Leviticus 20:10.

"If a man is found sleeping with another man's wife, both the man who slept with her and the woman must die." Deuteronomy 22:22

Is remarriage allowed?

In this situation, when divorce was allowed, so was remarriage. For these verses picture a woman being divorced, receiving her certificate of divorce, leaving the house and then being free to remarry.

Jesus' teaching on marriage and divorce

"When Jesus had finished saying these things, he left Galilee and went into the region of Judea to the other side of the Jordan. Large crowds followed him, and he healed them there. Some Pharisees came to him to test him. They asked, 'Is it lawful for a man to divorce his wife for any and every reason?'

'Haven't you read,' he replied, 'that at the beginning the Creator "made them male and female," and said, "For this reason a man will leave his father and mother and be united to his wife, and the two will become one flesh"? So they are no longer two, but one. Therefore what God has joined together, let man not separate.'

'Why then,' they asked, 'did Moses command that a man give his wife a certificate of divorce and send her away?'

Jesus replied, 'Moses permitted you to divorce your wives because your hearts were hard. But it was not this way from the beginning. I tell you that anyone who divorces his wife, except for marital unfaithfulness, and marries another woman commits adultery.'

The disciples said to him, 'If this is the situation between a husband and wife, it is better not to marry.'

Jesus replied, 'Not everyone can accept this word, but only those to whom it has been given. For some are eunuchs because they were born that way; others were made that way by men; and others have renounced marriage because of the kingdom of heaven. The one who can accept this should accept it.'"
Matthew 19:1-12

Jesus stresses the permanence of marriage

Before answering the Pharisees' question about divorce Jesus speaks about marriage. He refers them back to the first two chapters of Genesis. He underlines two facts:

- human sexuality was a divine creation
- human marriage was a divine ordinance.

Jesus puts Genesis 1:27 and Genesis 2:24 side by side and makes God the author of both texts. So the same Creator who "at the beginning…'made them male and female' also said in the biblical text, "For this reason a man will leave his father and mother and be united to his wife, and the two will become one flesh."

"So," adds Jesus, by way of explanation, "they are no longer two, but one."

Then Jesus adds his own prohibition, "Therefore what God has joined together let man not separate." The word for "joined together" here literally means "yoked together."

So Jesus teaches that marriage is no mere human contract. Marriage is a divine yoke! Marriage is something that was never intended to be broken.

Jesus says that divorce was allowed as a concession

Jesus taught that the Mosaic provision of divorce was a temporary concession to human sin.

After Jesus quoted verses from Genesis to the Pharisees they came up with their second question: "Why then did Moses command that a man give his wife a certificate of divorce and send her away?"

Jesus replied: "Moses permitted you to divorce your wives because your hearts were hard. But it was not this way from the beginning."

Note that what the Pharisees called a "command" Jesus refers to as a "permission." "Moses *permitted* you." Compare Matthew 19:7 with Matthew 19:8. Divorce was reluctantly allowed by God because of the stubbornness of human hearts. So it is wrong to think that God approved of divorce. The best that can be said about divorce is that it was a divine concession.

The Rabbis went wrong in their thinking when they ignored the important distinction between:

- God's absolute will, seen in Genesis 1 and 2
- God's legal provisions for human sinfulness, seen in Deuteronomy 24.

God's mercy is not the same as divine approval

In his commentary on this point, C. E. B. Cranfield says:

"Human conduct which falls short of the absolute command of God is sin and stands under the divine judgment. The provisions which God's mercy has designed for the limitation of the consequences of man's sin must not be interpreted as divine approval for sinning."

Jesus called remarriage after divorce "adultery"

If we ignore, for the moment, Jesus' exceptive clause and put together Jesus' teaching on marriage and divorce in the first three Gospels we have the following summary:

- A man who divorces his wife, and then remarries commits adultery.
- As it is assumed that his divorced wife will also remarry he causes her to commit adultery as well, Matthew 5:32.
- A woman who divorces her husband and then remarries is also committing adultery, Mark 10:12.
- A man who marries a divorcee commits adultery, and assuming reciprocity in this situation:
- A woman who marries a divorcee commits adultery.

This seems like very hard teaching, especially in our contemporary amoral society. But Jesus clearly teaches that if a divorce and a remarriage take place, which are not sanctioned by God, than any subsequent new union is adulterous. "If she divorces...and marries another man, she commits adultery" Mark 10:12.

Jesus allows for divorce and remarriage in one instance

Matthew 5:32 and 19:9 contain what has become known as the "exceptive clause."

"But I tell you that anyone who divorces his wife, except for marital unfaithfulness, causes her to become an adulteress" Matthew 5:32.

"I tell you that anyone who divorces his wife, except for marital unfaithfulness, and marries another woman commits adultery" Matthew 19:9.

These "exceptive clauses" were intended to exempt one category of divorce and remarriage from being called "adultery."

What does the word porneia mean?

The words "marital unfaithfulness" come from the Greek word *porneia*. According to the *Arndt-Gingrich Greek-English Lexicon of the New Testament*, *porneia* "includes every kind of unlawful sexual intercourse." *Porneia* means physical sexual immorality.

Jesus makes *porneia* the only permissible ground for divorce as it violates the "one flesh" principles laid down in Genesis.

Divorce is never mandatory

Divorce, on the ground of immorality, is permitted, but it is not required that it has to take place:

- Jesus never said that the innocent party must divorce his/her unfaithful partner.
- Jesus never said that unfaithfulness in itself destroys a marriage.
- Jesus is not even trying to encourage divorce on the grounds of unfaithfulness. Rather he is forbidding divorce in every other situation.

According to Jesus only illicit sexual relations, *porneia*, are grounds for which a marriage may be terminated.

Paul's teaching

In 1 Corinthians 7:10-16 the so-called "Pauline privilege" occurs.

To the married

"To the married I give this command (not I, but the Lord): A wife must not separate from her husband. But if she does, she must remain unmarried or else be reconciled to her husband. And a husband must not divorce his wife...But if the unbeliever leaves, let him do so."
1 Corinthians 7:10-11, 15

To the rest

"To the rest I say this (I, not the Lord): If any brother has a wife who is not a believer and she is willing to live with him, he must not divorce her. And if a woman has a husband who is not a believer and he is willing to live with her, she must not divorce him. For the unbelieving husband has been sanctified through his wife, and the unbelieving wife has been sanctified through her believing husband. Otherwise your children would be unclean, but as it is, they are holy.

But if the unbeliever leaves, let him do so. A believing man or woman is not bound in such circumstances; God has called us to live in peace. How do you know, wife, whether you will save your husband? Or, how do you know, husband, whether you will save your wife?" *1 Corinthians 7:12-16*

Paul underlines Jesus' teaching

Just as Jesus forbade divorce, so does Paul forbid divorce.

In 1 Corinthians 7:10-11, as in Romans 7:1-3, Paul echoes the teaching of Jesus recorded Mark and Matthew's Gospels. The teaching is put in absolute terms: "A wife must not separate from her husband...And a husband must not divorce his wife."

1. When no remarriage is allowed

In 1 Corinthians 7:10-11 Paul speaks about a wife who has separated from her husband not being allowed to divorce. "A wife must not separate from her husband. But if she does, she must remain unmarried or else be reconciled to her husband. And a husband must not divorce his wife."

The word Paul uses in these verses for "separate" *chorizo* does not mean divorce. The situation must be when the husband has *not* been unfaithful, so that the wife is not allowed to divorce him. Some other reason, which we are not told about, has prompted the wife to leave her husband. In such a situation Paul says that the separated wife is not free to remarry. Remarriage is not an option. She either has to be reconciled to her husband, or remain single.

2. What if an unbelieving partner deserts?

In 1 Corinthians chapter 7, in three successive paragraphs, Paul speaks to three different sets of people:

- In verses 8-9 he speaks to "the unmarried."
- In verses 10-11 he speaks to "the married."
- In verse 12-14 he speaks to "the rest."

From the context we can deduce that Paul is speaking about a particular kind of mixed marriage under the term "the rest."

For Paul does not allow a Christian to marry a non-Christian. He says a Christian woman "is free to marry anyone she wishes, but he must belong to the Lord," verse 39. The same is true of Christian men: see 2 Corinthians 6:14-15.

The situation Paul has in mind here is when a couple, both of whom are not Christians, marry, and subsequently one of them becomes a Christian.

Questions:

- What should the Christian partner do?
- Is the marriage unclean?
- And what about the children?
- Should the new Christian seek a divorce as soon as possible?

Paul's answer:

Paul answers this question by saying that if the unbelieving partner "is willing to live with" the believing partner, then the believing partner "must not divorce."

Paul says why this is the right action. He says that due to one of the couple becoming a Christian "the unbelieving husband has been sanctified through his wife, and the unbelieving wife has been sanctified through her believing husband."

What if the unbelieving partner wants a separation?

If the unbelieving partner wants to leave should the Christian wife do all she can to make him stay? Here Paul says, "if the

unbeliever leaves, let him do so. A believing man or woman is not bound in such circumstances" 1 Corinthians 7:15. Paul gives as his reason for this. It is because "God has called us to live in peace."

It is not that the believing partner should seek or desire a break-up of the marriage. Paul is saying that if the unbelieving partner takes the initiative and refuses to go on living with the Christian partner, then the believer is allowed to acquiesce to the partner's going.

Singleness

Why should anyone remain single?

- Because no one has proposed to you.
- Because you have not met anyone you want to propose to.
- Because you prefer to remain single.
- Because you have "renounced marriage because of the kingdom of heaven," Matthew 19:12.

Is there anything wrong in remaining single?

From the opening two chapters of Genesis it seems clear that marriage is God's plan for most of us. However, that does not mean to say that there is anything "second-rate" about being single.

Paul emphasized that being single is a gift from God, just as being married is God's gift. "Each man has his own gift from God; one has this gift, another has that gift." *1 Corinthians 7:7*

Are there any benefits to be derived from being single?

A person who is engaged in raising a family is not as free to serve the Lord as a single person. Paul amplifies this in 1 Corinthians 7:32-35:

1. Free from concern

"I would like you to be free from concern, as this world is passing away."

2. The affairs of the world versus the Lord's affairs

"An unmarried man is concerned about the Lord's affairs – how he can please the Lord. But a married man is concerned about the affairs of this world – how he can please his wife – and his interests are divided. An unmarried woman or virgin is concerned about the Lord's affairs: Her aim is to be devoted to the Lord in both body and spirit. But a married woman is concerned about the affairs of this world – how she can please her husband."

3. Undivided devotion to the Lord

"I am saying this for your own good, not to restrict you, but that you may live in a right way in undivided devotion to the Lord."

Are there any disadvantages in remaining single?

Unmarried people do not have the close companionship of one person or the possibility of enjoying sex with their married partner.

Paul gives this very down-to-earth advice to single people: "Now to the unmarried and the widows I say: It is good for them to stay unmarried, as I am. But if they cannot control themselves, they should marry, for it is better to marry than to burn with passion." *1 Corinthians 7:8-9*

Singleness and belonging to God's family

Some Christians are called to remain single and this should be respected. See Matthew 19:12. Some Christian fellowships concentrate so much on families that single Christians feel left out. Single people need to remember that they are members of God's family, just as married people are. Christian fellowships should be as keen to embrace single Christians as they are to provide for Christian families.

Being single in a church fellowship

"Within the life of the church, the paths of the single and the married should not be allowed to diverge. The shared life of the Christian community must become a context in which the differing gifts can be used for each other. There is much still to be learned about this. Are the homes of married Christians an added support for the single? Is the availability of the single Christian put at the disposal of his married friends, for "babysitting" duties and the like. And what is true of the mutual support of married and single needs to be true in a wider way of the care exercised by the married and the single for each other, so that nobody's home life becomes completely cut off from support and help." *Oliver O'Donovan, Regius Professor of Moral and Pastoral Theology at Oxford University*

Teenage sex: dating

Question:
Everyone seems to have a boyfriend or a girlfriend, so why shouldn't I?
Answer:
Did you know that over 50% of girls and over 40% of guys never date in high school?

Question:
Is there anything in the Bible about dating?
Answer:
We know that God wants the very best for us in every area of our lives. This includes relationships with boyfriends or girlfriends.

The Bible does give us principles to guide us in making decisions about dating.

1. Guard your heart.
The Bible warns us to be very careful about giving our affections.

"Above all else, guard your heart, for it is the wellspring of life." *Proverbs 4:23*

2. Who do we go around with?
We are not only known by the company we keep but we usually become like those we go around with. As usual, Paul can be relied on to tell us about this in quite a blunt way: "Do not be misled: 'Bad company corrupts good character.'" *1 Corinthians 15:33*

"He who walks with the wise grows wise,
  but a companion of fools suffers harm." *Proverbs 13:20*

3. What about "missionary dating"?
Christians dating non-Christians has been called "missionary dating." Does it really matter if Christians go out with non-Christians? The Christian answer on this is very unpopular but very straightforward: don't. Only date another Christian. See 2 Corinthians 6:14.

A prayer

To be honest, Lord,
Yes, I do like him.
And he likes me.
He hasn't actually said so
But I can tell.
He's really nice, Lord.
You'd like him!
He's kind, and helpful,
And intelligent and sporty,
And good at art –
And simply terrific on the guitar.
In fact you could say
He was re-a-lly dishy, Lord!
What do you say, Lord!
You like him?
O great…
But does he like you?
Well I don't think
I mentioned that early, did I?
No…
One thing he did say, I forgot.
No, Lord,
He doesn't like you.
Thank you for reminding me.
Loving you is the most important
Quality that my partner must have.

Teenage sex: how far is too far?

Question:
How far do you think it is right for
unmarried adults to go?
Answer:
Why do ask this question?

Question:
It's because I don't want to upset God, so
I need to know when I should stop.
Answer:
Wouldn't a better question be, "How can
I please God?" 2 Corinthians 5:9.

Another way of asking this question
would to say, "How can I put God first?"
Exodus 20:3; Matthew 19:29;
Luke 14:26, 33.

Another good question to ask is, "How
can I love God with all my heart, soul,
mind and strength? Luke 10:27.

Question:
But how can we know if we are loving
God?
Answer:
One simple way is by obeying God, that
is the way we love God, John 14:15; 1
John 5:3. For we are hardly showing our
love for him if we are happy to disobey
God when it suits us, 1 John 2:3, 4.

Question:
That still leaves me with the question
about how far can we go, as God has not
given us any rule book about this.
Answer:
That may be true. But God has given us
some helpful guidelines. One such
general principle is that whatever we do

in public or in private is seen by God,
Hebrews 4:14.

About your specific question about
"going too far" we could ask some of the
following questions:

- Would I be happy for younger
  Christians to follow my example in
  this?
- Would fellow-Christians approve of
  my actions? Matthew 18:6; 1
  Corinthians 11:1; Romans 14:15?
- Would I mind if what I was doing
  was made known in public?
- Am I treating the other person in the
  way that I would like my future wife
  or husband to be treated by
  someone else?
- Can I say that what I am doing is
  being beneficial to the other person
  in protecting, building up and
  honoring him/her?

Thoughts and actions
Question:
Didn't Jesus say that it was wrong even
to have lustful thoughts about a person?
And that if you do have such lustful
thoughts, that was as bad as adultery?
Answer:
Yes, he did, Matthew 5:28.

Question:
If that is the case we might as well go
the whole way. For that is no worse than
having lustful thoughts. Isn't that right?
Answer:
People have argued like this, saying that
if our imagination is equivalent to

action, then why not go the whole way? But this is muddled thinking. Jesus was saying that we should take sinful thoughts seriously, as seriously as sinful actions. We are meant to do this, not in order to indulge in both, but to abstain from both, Matthew 5:20; 1 Peter 2:11. If we don't do this we put ourselves in the same category as the Pharisees whom Jesus condemned, "On the outside you appear to people as righteous but on the inside you are full of hypocrisy" Matthew 23:28.

Teenage sex: contraception

Is more contraception really the answer?

Professor John Guillebaud, Professor of Family Planning at University College London, has proposed that girls of 12 should be fitted with a contraceptive implant that works for three years, with parents' consent, at the same time as their rubella injections.

Brook Advisory Clinics operate on the premise that teenage sex is both normal and desirable so long as it is engaged in "safely."

Caroline Woodruffe, long-time secretary of the Brook Advisory Clinics has said, "We try to get the parents to see that they should be pleased not shocked when children engage in sexual intercourse. We must be prepared to challenge our established attitudes that sexual activity in young people is dangerous. There are still too many workers in birth control clinics who believe consciously or subconsciously that sex before sixteen is sinful."

Is contraception a lesser evil?

"He who sins sexually sins against his own body" 1 Corinthians 6:18. Sexual sin always hurts someone.

- It shows that we opt for our own desires and not God's way. This hurts God.
- It often brings diseases to our bodies, so it hurts us.
- It may also deeply affect our personalities, so we are hurt again.

Promoting Christian values

Just what should Christians be affirming?

- Christians should affirm that sex is from God. It is a good gift and comes from the hands of a loving Creator: 1 Timothy 4:4.
- Christians should affirm that marriage is the only proper context for sex: Matthew 19:4-6.
- God has given us guidelines about how sex should be used.
- These guidelines are for our benefit and welfare.

Virginity

Virginity should be regarded as a virtue. It should be treasured.

Abstinence

Abstinence has never killed anyone. How terrible it is that so many people suffer so much and some die as a result of bad decisions over their sex lives.

Is abstinence the best policy?

The Bible teaches that marriage is the only place where God intends us to have sexual relationships, Genesis 2:24; Exodus 20:14.

Abstinence makes sense

Some medical journals in the United States regularly publish articles encouraging healthcare professionals to recommend abstinence. One such journal stated, "Abstinence is the

greatest sexual health promotion behavior available to Americans, especially to adolescents."
Postgraduate Medicine 1995; 97:121-34.

Fire

Sex is like fire. In your fireplace it can keep your house warm. But if fire gets out of control it can burn your house down. It can even kill you.

Sex is like that. Lots of people have now died of sexually transmitted diseases. Contemporary society may mock Christians for restricting sexual activity to marriage. But the best way to avoid sexually transmitted diseases is to limit your sex life to just one lifelong partner, who has not been infected with these diseases through promiscuity.

Numerous medical facts in support of God's ideal

"There are many medical arguments [as well as biblical ones] which indicate that premarital abstinence is the most effective response to the current decline in teenage sexual health."

Trevor Stammers, tutor in general practice at St George's Hospital Medical School, London

- Most pregnant teenagers have abortions.
- Casual sex puts people in serious danger, not only of HIV, but also of gonorrhea, chlamydia, and genital warts.

- Early intercourse often leads to subsequent regret.
- Young people who start having intercourse before they are 16 are three times more likely to become teenage parents than those who wait.

Won't contraception solve everything?

Many secular governments have contraception as the mainstay of their promotions about sexual health for adolescents. Clearly this fails, as about 80% of unplanned pregnancies come about as a result of failed contraception.

Getting pregnant and catching diseases are not the only ways that sex can hurt you. No one has invented a contraceptive against getting hurt.

"You didn't get pregnant. You didn't get AIDS. So why do you feel so bad?" says the first page of a leaflet produced by US Department of Health and Human Services.

Teenage sex: can premarital sex ever be okay?

Question:
"My boyfriend wants to have sex. I don't want to lose him. What should I do?"
Answer:
Are you sure premarital sex is wrong? When it comes to sex before marriage most people think that it may be okey for them, as there are exceptional circumstances for them. The Bible, however, teaches quite clearly that sex before marriage is against God's law. No exceptions are allowed for.

Question:
Doesn't this make God a spoil-sport?
Answer:
No. The prohibition about not having sex before marriage was laid down by God – for our good.

"It is God's will that you should be sanctified: that you should avoid sexual immorality; that each of you should learn to control his own body in a way that is holy and honorable, not in passionate lust like the heathen, who do not know God." *1 Thessalonians 4:3-5*

Sexual sin is something we should run away from, just as Joseph did when he was repeatedly approached by Potiphar's wife.

Paul wrote: "Flee from sexual immorality. All other sins a man commits are outside his body...your body is a temple of the Holy Spirit,...honor God with your body."
1 Corinthians 6:18-20

We are meant to be aiming at holiness, not sexual immorality. That is crystal clear in Ephesians 5:3: "But among you

there must not even be a hint of sexual immorality, or of any kind of impurity...because these are improper for God's holy people."

Question:
So where does all this leave me and my boyfriend?
Answer:
Ask yourself questions about your boyfriend: "Do you think that he's after your highest good, or his own pleasure? Does he want to obey God? Does he want you to obey God?"

In 1 Corinthians 13:5, we are told that love "is not self-seeking."

Also in verse 6 of 1 Corinthians 13 it says: "Love does not delight in evil but rejoices with the truth."

Dancing and dress

Remember Herodias' daughter

The beheading of John the Baptist is a good example of what dancing and immodesty can produce. On King Herod's birthday Herodias' daughter, Salome, pleased Herod as she danced before him. In his half-drunk state Herod said he would grant her any wish. Her mother told her to ask for John the Baptist's head. Read Matthew 14:1-11.

Shall we dance?

Dancing in itself is not always wrong. There are examples of dancing in the Bible in which it is used as a way to praise God, see Exodus 15:20-21; 2 Samuel 6:14. Dancing was also used in the Old Testament to express great rejoicing, see 1 Samuel 18:6. There are also examples of children dancing in the Bible, see Job 21:11; Luke 7:32.

So how can dancing ever be wrong?

The principle to guide us here is that it is wrong to lust in our hearts after others. "You have heard that it was said, 'Do not commit adultery.' But I tell you that anyone who looks at a woman lustfully has already commited adultery with her in his heart" Matthew 5:27-28. From this we deduce that it is also wrong to engage in any activity that excites such lusts in others. When this principle is applied to dancing it is not hard to see how some kinds of dancing are out for a Christian, while some other kinds of dancing can be wholesome.

Is there a Christian dress code?

The above principle about dancing also applies to how we dress. Any kind of clothes, or lack of clothes, which deliberately set out to be sexually provocative, should not be worn by unmarried Christians.

The apostle Peter contrasts two types of beauty. There is the outer "beauty" of being all dressed up, and there is inner beauty of character.

"Your beauty should not come from outward adornment, such as braided hair and the wearing of gold jewelry and fine clothes. Instead, it should be that of your inner self, the unfading beauty of a gentle and quiet spirit, which is of great worth in God's sight." *1 Peter 3:3-4*

What about masturbation and lust?

Roman Catholic teaching

Pope Paul VI issued a declaration in 1975 entitled: *Persona Humana - Declaration on Certain Questions Concerning Sexual Ethics.* Roman Catholics have historically taught that sexuality was designed only for procreation. So masturbation, as well as all forms of contraception, is deemed to be sinful.

"Masturbation constitutes a grave moral disorder..."

"Masturbation is an intrinsically and seriously disordered act...the deliberate use of the sexual faculty outside normal conjugal relations essentially contradicts the finality of the faculty."

"Even if it cannot be proved that Scripture condemns this sin by name, the tradition of the Church has rightly understood it to be condemned in the New Testament when the latter speaks of 'impurity,' 'unchasteness' and other vices contrary to chastity and continence."
Persona Humana - Declaration on Certain Questions Concerning Sexual Ethics

Bible teaching

Question:

Is there anything in the Bible about masturbation?

Answer:

No, it is never mentioned by name, and it is nowhere condemned. However, some people have argued from Genesis 38:8-10; Leviticus 15:16-17; Deuteronomy 23:10-11 that it is condemned. But the problem here is that these scriptures to not really apply to masturbation.

Some people think that masturbation is the unforgivable sin, but this is also quite wrong. The unforgivable sin is blasphemy against the Holy Spirit, Matthew 12:31.

But this does highlight the fact that for some Christians masturbation is a huge problem. They feel guilty and sinful, and ashamed that they are enslaved to such a habit, especially when they "give in" to masturbation.

General principles

The Bible has many principles that are relevant to masturbation. The issue here is lust, and what's going on in our minds, Colossians 3:5; 1 Peter 2:11; 1 John 2:16.

Although this runs counter to so much worldly advice about sex, Christians believe that we shouldn't just do what we like with our bodies. Even our bodies belong to God. And if we're married our bodies belong to our partners, 1 Corinthians 7:4.

Sexual fantasies

Some non-Christians have accused Christians of causing people to feel guilty about an innocent pleasurable activity. They argue that we should be free from such Victorian inhibitions.

As God has made us to be sexual beings what can be wrong with sexual fantasies? In Scripture illicit sexual fantasies are forbidden. If you wanted an argument against masturbation this is the best one.

The lustful look

In Matthew 5:28 Jesus said, "But I tell you that anyone who looks at a woman lustfully has already committed adultery with her in his heart." The word used for "look" in this verse does not mean a quick glance, but a prolonged stare.

The Old Testament teaches that adultery is wrong. Jesus went further and taught that indulging in lustful thoughts about adultery is also adultery. So if lustful thoughts are encouraged by masturbation then it is wrong. For example, some people look at pornographic magazines as they masturbate.

However, not everyone deliberately indulges in lustful thoughts during masturbation. If masturbation avoids mental sexual sin it cannot be categorized as a sin on the grounds of being full of lust. Some people argue that it is possible to use masturbation as a hedge against indulging one's sexual desires with another person, as it releases sexual tension.

Is there any way to defeat lustful thoughts, desires and actions?

Paul asks this same question: "Who will rescue me from this body of death?" Then he answers his own question by saying: "Thanks be to God – through Jesus Christ our Lord!" *Romans 7:22-24*

Feeding our minds and imaginations

Jesus taught that adultery starts in the heart and mind. We must not feed our minds on trash or on soft porn (or worse), which is all over the tabloids and in so many videos and TV channels and books and magazines. For out of the heart come all sorts of evils.

Chuck out evil

Think about one thing in your life that feeds your mind and imagination with lust. Take practical steps so this can be eradicated from your life.

"Turn my eyes away from worthless things; preserve my life according to your word" Psalm 119:37. Work out what you need to turn your eyes away from. And then do it. For the more we give ourselves over to sinful fantasies and pursuits, the more we become their slaves, Romans 6:16.

If you have any pornographic material in your possession, including computer files, chuck them out or delete them. Make no provision for your flesh. "Let us behave decently,...not in orgies and drunkenness, not in sexual immorality and debauchery." Romans 13:14. Stop stoking up the fire.

What should we think about?

Paul tells us what to think about.

"Finally, brothers, whatever is true, whatever is noble, whatever is right, whatever is pure, whatever is lovely, whatever is admirable – if anything is excellent or praiseworthy – think about such things.

Whatever you have learned or received or heard from me, or seen in me – put it into practice. And the God of peace will be with you."
Philippians 4:8-9

Love and lovers in the Bible

Question:
My wedding day has come. Are the emotions I'm now feeling for the person I'm madly in love with wrong and sinful?

Answer:
Not at all. To be bowled over emotionally and to be deeply attracted to someone else is part and parcel of being made in God's image. The Bible says that God himself has feelings. God has feelings of:

- love, Isaiah 43:4
- anger, Exodus 22:24
- grief, Genesis 6:6.

The four Gospels record that Jesus had many different emotions.

Question:
Are there any people in the Bible who felt in a state of total love?

Answer:
Yes, there a number of instances about people being madly in love in the Bible:

- Isaac and Rebecca, Genesis 24
- Jacob and Rachel, Genesis 29:16-30
- Boaz and Ruth, Ruth 3.

The Song of Songs

It is also quite reasonable to read this Old Testament book as a love poem.

The Song of Songs is a celebration of and an exulting in the love between a man and a woman. The language is very powerful and expressive. In it you'll find an outspoken and unashamed appreciation of physical attraction. It has

been called an erotic love poem.

Human sexual love is a wonderful gift from God. The fact that this book is included in the Bible shows that the physical aspect of marriage is something beautiful, precious and pure.

Bible verses for lovers

For the joy of love, read
Song of Songs 1:2, 4; 4:10; 7:6.

For the strength of love, read
Song of Songs 8:6.

For commitment to love, read
Song of Songs 2:16; 6:3; 7:10.

For the value of love, read
Song of Songs 8:7.

For verses about not treating love lightly, read Song of Songs 2:7. "Daughters of Jerusalem, I charge you by the gazelles and by the does of the field: Do not arouse or awaken love until it so desires." See also
Song of Songs 3:5; 8:4.

Is oral sex within marriage okay?

Question:
Is oral sex biblically wrong within a Christian marriage?

What the Bible says
The Bible does not discuss this specific activity. The Bible does not anywhere condemn it.

There is nothing to say that it is sinful. The Bible nowhere says that God is against a husband and wife expressing their love for each other in this way.

Christians believe that God is the author of sex and love. God intended the marriage relationship to be loving and joyful.

God also made us sensuous beings and inside marriage this can be expressed creatively so that both partners derive great pleasure from God's gift.

The Song of Songs
The Song of Songs is full of romantic language. It describes a beautiful, affectionate, romantic, sensuous, joyful and passionate love between husband and wife. Some would go so far as to say that it may be speaking about lovers tasting, eating and drinking of each other's bodies, Song of Songs 2:3; 4:16; 8:2.

Enjoying sex in marriage
Paul has some helpful words on this topic. "The husband should fulfil his marital duty to his wife, and likewise the wife to her husband...Do not deprive each other except by mutual consent." 1 Corinthians 7:3,5. From these verses it is clear that in a Christian marriage each partner should be glad "fulfill" their "marital duty" to each other.

Inside a Christian marriage the couple's bodies belong to each other. The wife's body now belongs to the husband. The husband's body now belongs to the wife.

There may well be times to abstain from sex. The example Paul gives is so that the couple can devote themselves to prayer. But Paul says this should be done:

- by mutual consent
- for a limited time

After that Paul says "come together again."

Contraception and treatment of infertility

Can contraception and treatment of infertility be justified on moral grounds? Assuming the context of a Christian marriage, what reasons are there for saying that contraception can be used to plan the size of our family? Can Christians use contraceptives with a clear conscience? Should Christian partners seek medical help if one or both of them are infertile?

WHAT DO ROMAN CATHOLICS SAY?

1. THEIR BASIC TEACHING

The basic Roman Catholic teaching is that contraception is wrong. And it is even wrong to teach about it, let alone introduce it, into any country, even where there is a desperate shortage of food and couples have very large families.

2. WHAT ABOUT ONAN?

Onan's example of practicing *coitus interruptus*, in Genesis 38:9 has been used to teach that any form of contraception is wrong. This is hardly a right interpretation of the verse. For what Onan did wrong was to avoid producing an heir with his deceased brother's wife. This action does not bear on the principle of avoiding pregnancy as such.

3. NO HELP AND NO HINDRANCE

Roman Catholics argue that it is natural for pregnancy to take place as a result of sexual intercourse, so to do anything to prevent this happening is "contrary to nature," and therefore wrong.

So it is both wrong to prevent pregnancy by any method of contraception and it is equally thought to be wrong to enhance fertility by artificial insemination (AID) or in vitro fertilization (IVF).

Traditional Roman Catholic teaching opposes any use of contraceptives or any use of artificial aids to assisting in child conception. The encyclical *Humanae Vitae* (1968) summarizes the Roman Catholic objections in this way: "The inseparable connection, willed by God and unable to be broken by man on his own initiative, between the two meanings of the conjugal act: the unitive meaning and the procreative meaning."

4. CONCESSIONS

There are three situations when Roman Catholics are allowed to engage in sexual intercourse, even though they know that it will not end in procreation.

When pregnancy cannot occur because the wife is post-menopausal, or already pregnant or where the couple are infertile it is not unlawful to have sexual intercourse.

As a result of understanding about the female reproductive cycle and in particular the process of ovulation, in 1952 Pope Pius XII and again in 1968 Pope Paul VI gave permission for the so-called "rhythm" or "natural" method to be used by married couples.

Stewardship

The basic argument used by Christians who oppose the Roman Catholic view on this topic is the biblical teaching about stewardship. According to Genesis 1:28, God gave the responsibility to men and women to manage the rest of creation and its resources: "God blessed them and said to them, 'Be fruitful and increase in number; fill the earth and subdue it. Rule over the fish of the sea and the birds of the air and over every living creature that moves on the ground.'"

Adam and Eve, in the context of an underpopulated world, were told to "be fruitful and increase in number."

Two deductions

1. Help is okay

Clearly it is God's will for married couples to procreate. Therefore it seems reasonable to deduce from this that it is quite right and proper to make use of advanced medical technology to help any men and women who are less than fertile for some reason.

2. Contraceptives are okay

The second deduction is that it is right to view modern contraceptive technology as a gift from God and to limit the size of our families. This is especially relevant in our very overcrowded world.

Surrogacy and types of contraception

A hesitation over surrogacy

What about surrogacy? As this is a means to provide childless couples with the joy of a baby, why should Christians have any hesitations about it?

The teaching that the Bible provides on the subject of creation quite rightly leads to a Christian appreciation of human value and dignity. We recall that men and women are still in God's image, so it would be wrong to use people as means to an end.

In surrogacy (male or female) a semen donor or a surrogate mother is used so a couple can achieve parenthood. The moral hesitation about, or outright rejection of, this method of childbirth is that it is possible to say that the third party is demoted, and relegated to being a mere spermator or womb-leaser.

Are all methods of contraception morally okey?

If we agree that human life starts at fertilization what implications to the different methods of contraception have for Christians?

Two categories of contraception

Left apart, the human egg and the sperm soon disintegrate. But a fertilized egg, given the necessary environment, will develop into one of us. This clearly divides the different methods of contraception into two camps. There are those methods that prevent eggs and sperms from ever meeting, and there are those methods that destroy the microscopic, newly formed human life.

So reversible barrier methods, such as diaphragms, caps, condoms (with or without spermicidals) and the more irreversible male or female voluntary sterilization fall into the former category and present no moral problems for most Christians.

What is called contraception, such as the "morning-after-pill" is strictly speaking not contraception at all, but abortion. What "morning-after-pills" are doing cannot be morally justified. Nor can very early abortion, so-called menstrual extraction or regulation be morally justified. Any method of killing a fertilized egg or fetus is an abortion.

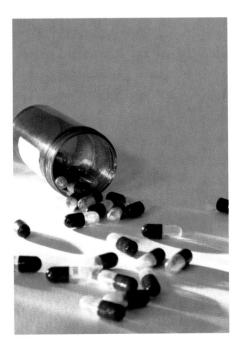

Can Christians make use of advances in infertility treatments?

Developments in human fertilization

The first use of donor sperm to treat infertility was not achieved until 1978 when the first IVF live birth took place. This was due to the work of Robert Edwards and Patrick Steptoe. They were responsible for the first "test tube" baby.

Common practice

The ability to produce embryos in a laboratory has now made the following practices common:

- Embryos are created for research from the eggs of living or dead donors.
- Abortifacient so-called "contraceptives" are available. This refers to any procedure that takes place after fertilization.
- Embryos are frozen for fertility treatment.
- Embryos are now widely used in fertility, contraceptive and genetic research.
- Genetic testing and disposal of abnormal embryos is now widespread.

How should we view the use of the human embryo in medical research?

The Declaration of Geneva, 1948, lays down that doctors "should maintain the utmost respect for human life from the time of conception."

The Declaration of Helsinki, 1975, states that in biomedical research "the interest of science and society should never take precedence over considerations related to the well-being of the subject."

Clearly the present use and disposal of human embryos in medical research go against these principles. This is primarily because human embryos are not treated as if they have the status of human beings.

Stem cells and embryos

The argument goes that if stem cells of an embryo are used we may have a means of helping or curing a disease such as Alzheimer's disease. Who dare oppose that? But there is an insuperable moral barrier against experimenting on embryos. It boils down to using some helpless human beings as a means of

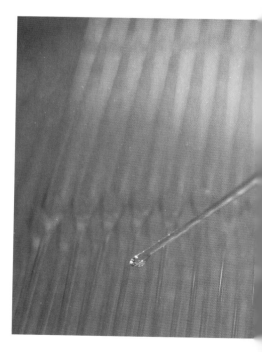

gaining happiness for others.

All embryo experimentation should be banned, and alternative medical means worked on to produce similar beneficial results.

Contraception

Abortifacient contraceptives are now widely used. These are contraceptives that usually aim to prevent the implantation of an already fertilized egg. Many doctors regard them as part of the "full range of family planning services."

Treatment of infertility

In many countries up to one in nine couples are infertile in some way. Today

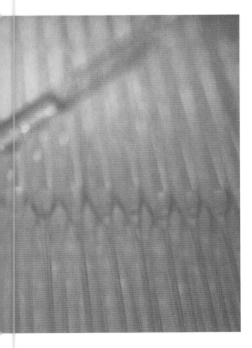

there are various tests available to diagnose the problem. The following treatments are being more and more common:

- artificial insemination by husband
- artificial insemination by donor sperm
- intracytoplasmic sperm injection (ICSI)
- ovarian stimulation with drugs
- fallopian tube surgery
- *in vitro* fertilization (IVF)
- gamete intrafallopian transfer (GIFT).

These procedures result in hundreds of thousands embryos being used for research. Many thousands of unused frozen embryos are destroyed.

Prenatal diagnosis

It is now common practice for pregnant women to have tests that indicate the medical health of their unborn baby. Diagnosis of genetic diseases by amniocentesis, at 16 weeks, and chorion villus biopsy, at eight weeks, are no longer unusual.

The way that this is commonly expressed is that this gives the parents the opportunity to make "an informed decision" about continuing the pregnancy or terminating it. The rights of the unborn baby are rarely referred to. For example, in Britain nine out of ten unborn babies who are diagnosed as having Down's syndrome are now aborted.

Biblical principles and human fertility

What are the biblical principles that apply to these medical practices?

In the areas of contraception, infertility treatments and genetics Christian medical practitioners as well as Christian couples need to be guided in the decisions they make by the principles laid down in Scripture.

1. The Sovereignty of God

- God created human life in his own image, Genesis 1:27.
- Children are a gift from God, Psalm 127:3-5; 128:3-4.
- God opens the wombs of the infertile, Genesis 30:22; 1 Samuel 1:19-20.
- God "settles the barren woman in her home as a happy mother of children," Psalm 113:9.

2. The responsibility of stewardship

God has given us the responsibility to be stewards of his creation and this validates scientific enquiry and application. However, this should always be carried out for the good of individual human beings. From this it follows that people engaged in medical research and practice should use their God-given skills to alleviate infertility where this is possible and to minimize the risk of genetic disease where this is appropriate. However, Christians believe that all such work should be carried out under the umbrella of God's revealed standards of right and wrong. For the Christian the end does not justify the means.

3. God's grace

Christians have received God's grace and forgiveness and it is our duty to be compassionate towards everyone who suffers. In the present discussion this applied to all who suffer as a result of being childless and who suffer from genetic diseases.

The pain of childlessness is understood by God. Rachel said to Jacab, "Give me children, or I'll die!" Genesis 30:1.

Isaac, Joseph, Samson, Samuel and John the Baptist were all born to initially infertile couples.

4. The sanctity of life

Christians believe that it is right to protect unborn, innocent human life. For all human life is made in God's image Genesis 9:6,7.

One relevant principle here is that the strong are meant to make sacrifices for the weak, rather than the weak being sacrificed, that is, killed, by the strong, Philippians 2:5-8.

The status of the embryo is the key issue in contraception, infertility and genetics.

If we believe that embryos are fully human we should treat them as such and so not use those contraceptives, infertility treatments or genetic interventions that would put their survival at risk.

But if we believe that embryos are disposable we may have no objection to these procedures.

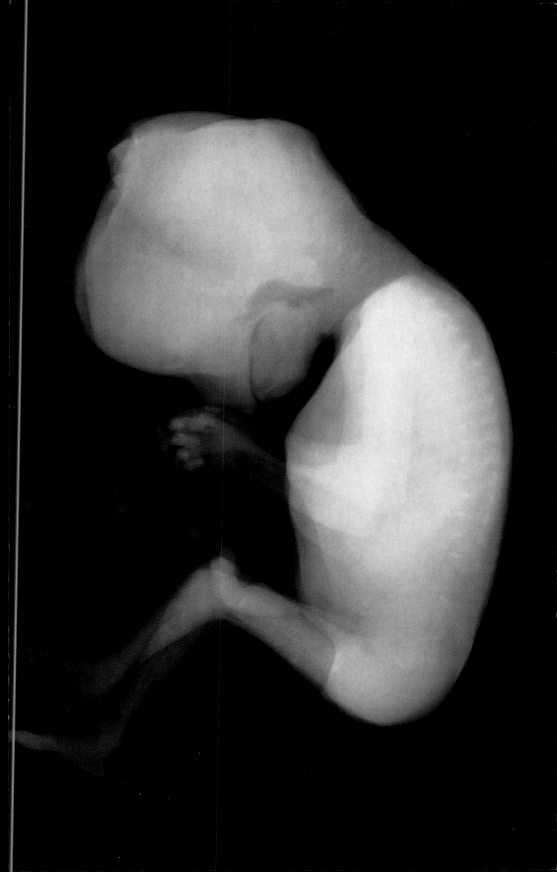

The Bible and prenatal life

Biblical arguments for the worth of prenatal life

1. Human beings are made in the image of God.
2. Human beings should not be unjustly killed.
3. All human life is equally valuable.
4. The weak should be especially cared for.
5. The Bible often mentions and refers to prenatal life.

Corollary

It follows from the above principles that nothing should be done to an embryo that we would not be justified in doing to another human being. Prenatal life is human life.

Very early human life

1. The argument that embryos are not fully human

This is often advanced by secular philosophers and biologists.

The "evidence"

Embryos do not have rationality and do not have the capacity for relationships. The neural crest does not appear until day 10.

A reply

The value of a human being does not depend on its capacities or attributes. The value of a human being lies in the fact that it is human.

The "evidence"

About 40-70% of embryos never reach maturity. Given this very high mortality of early embryos, why should Christians take such pains in trying to protect them?

A reply

The value of human beings is not measured by their survival rates. Even where survival rates are low this gives us no mandate to end their lives prematurely.

The "evidence"

Lots of embryos are abnormal and abort spontaneously. So why not make tests for abnormalities and abort the abnormal?

A reply

The value of human beings is not measured by their level of normality. Just because one detects an abnormal embryo that does not mean to say that we should kill it.

The "evidence"

Sperm and ova are alive but nobody says that they are human. So why should anyone call a microscopic "blob" human?

A reply

Totally unlike sperm and ova an embryo is a genetically distinct human being. They have a unique genotype. They also have the ability to grow.

The "evidence"
Two sperm may form an "organism" as in a hydatidiform mole.

A reply
But a hydatidiform mole is not a human being. It was not formed from the union of a male and female but rather by two male gametes.

The "evidence"
Conception can be thought of a process. It can be said not to be complete until the first cell division, or even until it is implanted.

A reply
Even if you call conception a process, it still begins at fertilization. After that we have no right to interrupt this process at any point. You could say that "life" is a process; does that give us the right to end it?

The "evidence"
We don't treat embryos like human beings, in that we don't baptize them, or mourn their loss.

A reply
The value of an embryo is not dependent on what or how *we* think of them but on how *God* thinks of them.

Conclusion
We should never treat embryos as if they were expendable, even if people engaged in medical research do.

Single sex issues: homosexuality and lesbianism

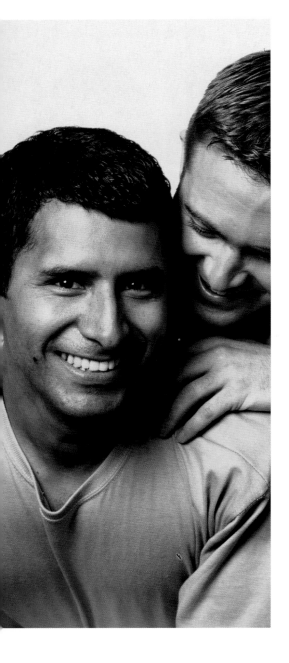

Right and wrong
In today's easy-going society any group of people who say that some things are definitely wrong often get a bad press. Christians, for example, believe that the clear teaching of the Bible enables us to conclude that nobody should marry someone of the same sex.

No sin and no temptation
However, if you think that it's okey for two gay men, or two lesbians to be married then you will not think that you are being tempted to do anything wrong if you desire to follow that way of life. It is because Christians believe that such a way of living is wrong that they say that Christians are being tempted to live in a sinful way to even contemplate a gay marriage, see 1 Peter 5:8-9.

An alternative lifestyle
The practice of homosexuality was once regarded as some kind of sinister perversion. Now it is becoming more and more accepted as an alternative lifestyle. As a result a number of countries are now changing their laws so that homosexuals and lesbians have the same rights as heterosexual couples.

The number of gay churches has recently greatly increased.

Some people who are openly gay are now ordained and become ministers in major Protestant denominations.

A number of cities such as San Francisco and Key West are known as "gay" cities.

What is the right Christian response?
1. Not homophobia
Christians are often accused of being homophobic in their reactions to gay people. On some occasions they have been accused of "gay bashing."

Jesus told us not to pass judgment on others, even though we are also required to speak the truth in love, Ephesians 4:15.

"However strongly we may disapprove of homosexual practices, we have no liberty to dehumanize those who engage in them." *John Stott*

2. Helping those who want to overcome homosexuality
Jesus was always quick to receive sinners. But he always pointed them in the way of righteousness and life everlasting. Jesus is our role model and we should follow his example in this.

Jesus did not condemn the woman caught in the very act of adultery, John 8:2-11, but he also helped her by telling her to give up her lifestyle of adultery: "Then neither do I condemn you...Go now and leave your life of sin."
John 8:11

3. Gentleness
Qualities such as gentleness are so often all too conspicuous by their absence when it comes to Christians speaking out against what they believe to be wrong. But the apostle Paul counseled, "A servant of the Lord must not quarrel but be *gentle* to all" 2 Timothy 2:24.

Paul on counseling
Paul advised the Christians at Galatia how to approach the tricky situation of helping a Christian who had gone astray: "Brethren, if a man is overtaken in any trespass, you who are spiritual restore such a one in a spirit of gentleness, considering yourself lest you also be tempted. Bear one another's burdens, and so fulfill the law of Christ."
Galatians 6:1, 2

Again we note the emphasis on the *spirit of gentleness.*

Is homosexuality an illness?
It used to be regarded as a form of mental illness but this is no longer the case.

Is homosexuality a sin?
In some old Bible dictionaries homosexuality is linked with "sexual perversion."

There are a number of verses in the Bible that condemn the practice of homosexuality.

"Do not lie with a man as one lies with a woman; that is detestable," Leviticus 18:22.

"Because of this, God gave them over to shameful lusts. Even their women exchanged natural relations for unnatural ones. In the same way the men also abandoned natural relations with women and were inflamed with lust for one another. Men committed indecent acts with other men, and received in themselves the due penalty for their perversion," Romans 1:26-27.

Other relevant scriptures are: Genesis 19:1-13; Judges 19; Leviticus 20:13; Romans 1:18-25; 28-32; 1 Corinthians 6:9,10; 1 Timothy 1:8-11.

Just as there are specific biblical bans on prostitution, pre-marital intercourse and adultery, so there are specific biblical bans on homosexual behavior. See 1 Corinthians 6:13-18; Ephesians 5:3; 1 Thessalonians 4:3; Exodus 20:14. "Men commited indecent acts with other men." Romans 1:27.

Question:
What you think about homosexual sex?
Answer:
The Bible teaches that homosexual sex is out, Genesis 19:1-13; Judges 19; Leviticus 18:22; 20:13; Romans 1:18-32; 1 Corinthians 6:9, 10; 1 Timothy 1:8-11.

Question:
Do you mean to say that even if both partners want homosexual sex, and even if they are very strongly emotionally bonded to each other, and even if they are not at all attracted to the opposite sex, they still can't have sex with each other?
Answer:
Yes, that is exactly right.

Question:
So what should I do if I have overwhelmingly strong feelings for someone of my own sex?

Answer:
The Bible teaches that these feelings should not be acted on. See Genesis 19:1-13; Judges 19; Romans 1:18-32.

Question:
Are you ruling out same sex deep friendship and companionship?
Answer:
No, of course not. John 13:1, 34, 35; 1 Samuel 18:1-3; 2 Samuel 1:26. We all know about the deep friendship between David and Jonathan. It was said to surpass the love a man has for a woman. But there is no hint of any homosexual sex here. "I grieve for you Jonathan my brother;...Your love for me was wonderful, more wonderful than that of a woman." 2 Samuel 1:26.

The straightforward teaching of the Bible boils down to: No sex except in the context of a lifelong, monogamous, heterosexual relationship. This means no sex outside marriage.

The traditional view
In Christian circles homosexuality has traditionally been regarded as a sin. So the state of being "homosexual" was thought to be abnormal, unnatural and totally unacceptable.

Today, Christians are keen to point out that we are all human beings, and that we are all sinners, and that it is quite wrong to put some people in a category on their own as if they were the worst sinners in the world.

"In God's view I suspect we are all

sexual deviants. I doubt if there is anyone who has not had a lustful thought that deviated from God's perfect ideal of sexuality." *Dr Merville Vincent, of the Department of Psychiatry at Harvard Medical School*

An important distinction?

Today, many evangelical Christians make a distinction between homosexual sex, which is sinful, and the condition or orientation of a person.

"Contemporary use of 'homosexual' to describe those who experience sexual 'desire' for others of the same sex is not primary in Scripture. Nearly every reference is to actual performance of sex acts with a person or persons of the same sex." *The Applied Bible Dictionary, Fleming H. Revell Co, 1990*

Among Christians who adhere to the authority of the Bible a minority believe that the Bible does not condemn loving homosexual relationships.

Feminism

The abuse and downgrading of women

Few would disagree that over the centuries women have been badly treated, mistreated and even treated as goods and chattels and often abused.

- How could it have been right for men only to have the vote?
- How could it have been right for men only to be doctors?
- How could it have been right for men only to go to university and gain degrees?

A history of being wronged

This is no recent phenomenon.

IMPERFECT MALES

"Females are imperfect males, accidently produced by the father's inadequacy or by the malign influence of a moist south wind."
Aristotle

DEFECTIVE

"As regards the individual nature, woman is defective and misbegotten, for the active power of the male seed tends to the production of a perfect likeness in the masculine sex; while the production of a woman comes from defect in the active power."
Thomas Aquinas

NOT TO RULE

"To promote a woman to rule any realm or city is repugnant to nature."
John Knox

A THING

"In Jewish law a woman was not a person but a thing." *William Barclay*
Each morning a Jewish man thanked God that he had not made him "a Gentile, a slave or a woman."

VOTING

"Nothing could be more anti-Biblical than letting women vote." *Editorial, Harper's Magazine, November 1853*

INFERIOR

"A woman is inferior to man in every way." *Josephus*

EXPLOITATION

"Women: Men have authority over women because Allah has made the one superior to the other. As for those whom you fear disobedience, admonish them and send them to beds apart and beat them." *Koran*

WOMEN'S MINISTRY

"If the Bible teaches the equality of women, why does the church refuse to ordain women to preach the gospel, to fill the offices of deacons and elders, and to administer the sacraments?"
Elizabeth Cady Stanton, 1895

"I believe that there are situations in which it is entirely appropriate for women to teach, and to teach men, provided that in so doing they are not usurping an improper authority over them." *John Stott*

Are men and women equal in God's sight?

The key Bible verses here are Genesis 1:26-28. In these verses are found:

- God's wish:
  "Let us make man…and let them rule." The word "man" here and often elsewhere in the Bible refers to humankind, to both men and women. So when God says "Let us make man" it means, "Let us make men and women."
- God's creation:
  "So God created man in his own image, in the image of God he created him; male and female he created them."
- God's blessing:
  "Be fruitful…fill the earth and subdue it."

Three truths about men and women

- God made men and women in his own image.
- God made men and women so they could have children.
- God made men and women to rule over his creation and other creatures. Men and women were both created by God and both had God's image.

No male or female

Paul wrote: "There is neither Jew nor Greek, slave nor free, male nor female, for you are all one in Christ Jesus" Galatians 3:28. So in God's sight men and women are equal. In no sense is one sex superior or inferior to the other.

Genesis 2:18-22

"No male or female" does not mean that there are no differences between men and women. Men and women are equal but not identical. As J. H. Yoder has written, "equality of *worth* is not identity of *role*."

This is taught in Genesis 2:18-22 where the complementarity of men and women is seen.

Equal

God has given equal dignity to men and women. So men and women can respect each other, love each other, serve each other, but never despise each other.

Complementary

God created men and women so that they are complementary to each other. So men and women are to respect each other's differences.

Adultery

Adultery is committed when a married person has a sexual relationship with somebody they are not married to, and when an unmarried person has a sexual relationship with a married person.

In the world's media adultery is endlessly promoted and glamorized. It rarely accurately portrays the heartache adultery so often causes.

Why is God against adultery?

1. Adultery hurts the one who was betrayed by adultery.
2. To allow adultery would make every marriage insecure.
3. Adultery hurts the children of the marriage.
4. Adultery is expensive, paying divorce lawyers.
5. Adultery means breaking important promises.

Holiness

God's will is for us to be holy, which includes avoiding sexual immorality.

"It is God's will
that you should be sanctified:
that you should avoid sexual
   immorality;
that each of you should learn to
   control his own body in a way that is
holy and
honorable,
not in passionate lust like the heathen,
   who do not know God."
1 Thessalonians 4:3, 4

Thoughts as well as actions

- Watch your thoughts; they become words.
- Watch your words; they become actions.
- Watch your actions; they become habits.
- Watch your habits; they become character.
- What your character; for it becomes your destiny.

That applies to thoughts and actions concerning sexual relationships. "You have heard that it was said, 'Do not commit adultery.' But I tell you that anyone who looks at a woman lustfully has already committed adultery with her in his heart." *Matthew 5:27, 28*

Old Testament teaching on adultery

Bible teaching about adultery in the words of the Bible

The Bible's teaching about adultery shows how Jesus' own teaching was in line with the Old Testament and how Jesus' teaching always focused on inner motives.

The Old Testament
The books of the law

JOSEPH RUNS AWAY

Now Joseph was well-built and handsome, and after a while his master's wife took notice of Joseph and said, "come to bed with me!"

But he refused. "How...could I do such a wicked thing?"

She caught him by his cloak and said, "Come to bed with me!" But he left his cloak in her hand and ran out of the house.
Genesis 39:6, 7, 9, 12

THE TEN COMMANDMENTS

"You shall not commit adultery."
Exodus 20:14

RESTITUTION REQUIRED

"If a man seduces a virgin who is not pledged to be married and sleeps with her, he must pay the bride-price, and she shall be his wife. If her father absolutely refuses to give her to him, he must still pay the bride-price for virgins."
Exodus 22:16, 17

NEIGHBORS

"Do not have sexual relations with your neighbor's wife and defile yourself with her."
Leviticus 18:20

PUNISHMENT

"If a man sleeps with a woman who is a slave girl promised to another man but who has not been ransomed or given her freedom, there must be due punishment. Yet they are not to be put to death, because she had not been freed."
Leviticus 19:20

A WARNING TO PARENTS

"Do not degrade your daughter by making her a prostitute, or the land will turn to prostitution and be filled with wickedness."
Leviticus 19:29

SEVERE PUNISHMENT

"If a man commits adultery with another man's wife – with the wife of his neighbor – both the adulterer and the adulteress must be put to death."
Leviticus 20:10

DISHONOR

"If a man sleeps with his father's wife, he has dishonored his father. Both the man and the woman must be put to death; their blood will be on their own heads."
Leviticus 20:11

PERVERSION

"If a man sleeps with his father's wife...If a man sleeps with his daughter-in-law, both of them must be put to death. What they have done is a perversion; their blood will be on their own heads." *Leviticus 20:11, 12*

AN UNAMBIGUOUS COMMAND

"You shall not commit adultery." *Deuteronomy 5:18*

GOD'S PEOPLE

"No Israelite man or woman is to become a shrine prostitute." *Deuteronomy 23:17*

The book of Proverbs

ADULTERY LEADS TO DEATH

"It will save you also from the adulteress, from the wayward wife with her seductive words, who has left the partner of her youth and ignored the covenant she made before God. For her house leads down to death and her paths to the spirits of the dead. None who go to her return or attain the paths of life." *Proverbs 2:16-19*

- *Entrapment:* see Proverbs 5:3-9.
- *God sees adultery:* see Proverbs 5:20-22.
- *Fire:* see Proverbs 6:24-32.

Hosea

SPIRITUAL ADULTERY

"When the Lord began to speak through Hosea, the Lord said to him, 'Go, take to yourself an adulterous wife and children of unfaithfulness, because the land is guilty of the vilest adultery in departing from the Lord.'" *Hosea 1:2*

New Testament teaching on adultery

Jesus' teaching about adultery

- *The lustful stare:* see Matthew 5:27-28.
- *Divorce and adultery:* see Matthew 5:32.
- *The origin of adultery:* see Matthew 15:19.
- *Remarriage and adultery:* see Matthew 19:9.
- *Jesus reinforces the Ten Commandments:* see Matthew 19:18.
- *Jesus and the adulteress:* see John 8:4-11.

The rest of the New Testament

REMARRIAGE

"For example, by law a married woman is bound to her husband as long as he is alive, but if her husband dies, she is released from the law of marriage. So then, if she marries another man while her husband is still alive, she is called an adulteress. But if her husband dies, she is released from that law and is not an adulteress, even though she marries another man." *Romans 7:2,3*

AVOID THE IMMORAL

"But now I am writing you that you must not associate with anyone who calls himself a brother but is sexually immoral or greedy, an idolater or a slanderer, a drunkard or a swindler. With such a man do not even eat." *1 Corinthians 5:11*

MALE PROSTITUTES

"Do you not know that the wicked will not inherit the kingdom of God? Do not be deceived: Neither the sexually immoral nor idolaters nor adulterers nor male prostitutes nor homosexual offenders nor thieves nor the greedy nor drunkards nor slanderers nor swindlers will inherit the kingdom of God. And that is what some of you were. But you were washed..." *1 Corinthians 6:9-11*

THE BODY IS FOR THE LORD

"'Food for the stomach and the stomach for food' – but God will destroy them both. By his power God raised the Lord from the dead, and he will raise us also. The body is not meant for sexual immorality, but for the Lord, and the Lord for the body. Do you not know that your bodies are members of Christ himself? Shall I then take the members of Christ and unite them with a prostitute? Never! Do you not know that he who unites himself with a prostitute is one with her in body? For it is said, 'The two will become one flesh.' But he who unites himself with the Lord is one with him in spirit. Flee from sexual immorality. All other sins a man commits are outside his body, but he who sins sexually sins against his own body." *1 Corinthians 6:13-18*

IMMORALITY AND GREED

"But among you there must not be even a hint of sexual immorality, or of any kind of impurity, or of greed, because these are improper for God's holy people. Nor should there be obscenity, foolish talk or coarse joking, which are out of place, but rather thanksgiving. For of this you can be sure: No immoral, impure or greedy person – such a man is an idolater – has any inheritance in the kingdom of Christ and of God."
Ephesians 5:3-5

HONOR MARRIAGE

"Marriage should be honored by all, and the marriage bed kept pure, for God will judge the adulterer and all the sexually immoral."
Hebrews 13:4

Speaking out

Christians are sometimes characterized as being killjoys and for condemning everything that is pleasurable. John the Baptist was so outspoken, for condemning Herod for marrying his brother's wife while his brother was still alive, that he was beheaded for his pains, "Now Herod had arrested John and bound him and put him in prison because of Herodias, his brother Philip's wife, for John had been saying to him: 'It is not lawful for you to have her.'"
Matthew 14:1-12.

THE SINFUL NATURE

"The acts of the sinful nature are obvious: sexual immorality, impurity and debauchery;...and envy; drunkenness, orgies, and the like. I warn you, as I did before, that those who live like this will not inherit the kingdom of God."
Galatians 5:19, 21

Quotations on adultery

SEPARATION

"If a husband, separated from his wife, approaches another woman, he is an adulterer because he makes that woman commit adultery; and the woman who lives with him is an adulteress, because she has drawn another's husband to herself."
Basil the Great

JEWS AND ADULTERY

"Every Jew must die before he will commit idolatry, murder or adultery."
Rabbinic saying

ADULTERY AND GOD'S WILL

"Adultery is a sin and is opposed to the will of God and to all that is pure in body, mind and heart."
W. H. Griffith Thomas

ADULTERY IN THE MIND AND HEART

"There are highly respectable men and women who would never dream of committing an act of adultery, but look at the way in which they enjoy sinning in the mind and in the imagination. We are dealing with practical matters, we are dealing with life as it is...How often do men sin by reading novels and biographies. You read the reviews of a book and find that it contains something about a man's misconduct or behavior, and you buy it. We pretend we have a general philosophical interest in life, and that we are sociologists reading out of pure interest. No, no; it is because we love the thing; we like it. It is sin in the heart; sin in the mind!"
Martyn Lloyd-Jones

Fornication

Fornication is...

Fornication is when two unmarried people have a sexual relationship. Pre-marital sex is a form of fornication.

Defining fornication

Fornication, in Hebrew *zanah*, in Greek, *porneia*, is voluntary sexual intercourse between a man and woman who are not married to each other.

Adultery, sexual intercourse with a married person, is one type of fornication.

As far as God's people, the Israelites, were concerned, every kind of fornication was roundly condemned: Leviticus 21:9; 19:29; Deuteronomy 22:20, 21, 23-29; 23:18; Exodus 22:16.

The teaching about fornication is just as clear in the New Testament. See Matthew 5:32; 19:9; John 8:41; Acts 15:20, 29; 21:25; Romans 1:29; 1 Corinthians 5:1; 6:13, 18; 7:2; 10:8; 2 Corinthians 12:21; Galatians 5:19; Ephesians 5:3; Colossians 3:5; 1 Thessalonians 4:3; Jude 1:7; Revelation 2:14, 20-21; 9:21; 14:8; 17:2, 4.

An inclusive word

The Greek word *porneia* included any sexual sin committed before or after marriage. So "fornication" included any sexual activity outside marriage. And this meant not only premarital sex, but also adultery, homosexual acts, incest, remarriage after unbiblical divorce, and bestiality, all of which are explicitly forbidden in the law as given through

Moses, Leviticus 20:10-21.

Jesus enlarged the prohibition against adultery to include lust, Matthew 5:28.

Sometimes, the word "fornication" is used in a symbolic sense in the Bible. Then it means forsaking God or following idols, Isaiah 1:2; Jeremiah 2:20; Ezekiel 16; Hosea 1:2; 2:1-5; Jeremiah 3:8, 9.

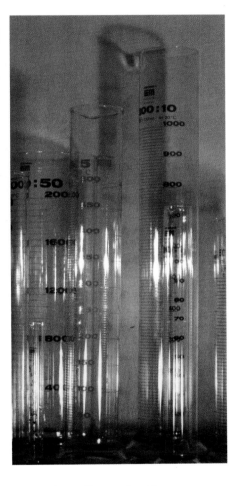

Fornication sells you short in many ways

If the relationship breaks up, which it most often does, one of you is going to be badly hurt. Despite what people say about having a kind of "trial marriage" fornication robs you of some of the joy of marriage. Fornication leaves you open to catching sexually transmitted diseases. From these you may even die.

Question:
Lots of people today go in for "trial" marriages. Are you going to condemn all those who live together and/or sleep together, just because they are unmarried?

Answer:
If unmarried people have sex with each other the Bible does not mince its words. It call this fornication, Exodus 22:16, 17; Deuteronomy 22:13-21; 1 Corinthians 6:9; Ephesians 5:31, 32. Sex is meant to be kept inside the relationship of marriage.

Question:
Why does Christian teaching about sex seem so negative?

Answer:
Negatives can be very positive. God's prohibitions are always meant for our good and our welfare. In that way "no" should be seen as a positive. Have you ever thought how our world would be if sex was kept inside marriage? There would be almost:

- no unwanted pregnancies
- no abortions
- no STDs (sexually transferrable diseases),
- no AIDS
- no tubal infertility
- no cervical cancer.

Somebody once said that "'No' is the best oral contraceptive, the best immunization and the best way to stay happy and healthy."

Abortion

1. What does the Bible say about abortion?

The word "abortion" is nowhere to be found in a Bible concordance. But the Bible does speak about:

- the value of life in the womb, Psalm 139:13-16
- intentional killing, Exodus 21:12
- the practice of child sacrifice, Leviticus 20:2; Deuteronomy 12:31, 22:2, 3.

2. WHAT IS "PRO-LIFE"?

The pro-life argument may be defined as follow

- The unborn entity is fully human from the moment of conception.
- Abortion results in the intentional death of the unborn entity.
- So, abortion entails the intentional killing of a human being.
- This killing is in the vast majority of instances is totally unjustified.
- For the unborn human being has a full right to life.

Exception

Where there is a high probability that a woman's pregnancy will result in her own death, as is the case with a tubal pregnancy, then abortion is justified.

The moral grounds for this hang on the principle that it is a greater good that one human should live, in this case the mother, rather than that two human beings should die, in this case the mother and the child.

3. What about abortion after of rape or incest? Is it then justifiable?

Pregnancies from the horrific acts of rape and incest are small.

"A number of studies have shown that pregnancy resulting from rape is very uncommon. One study, looking at 2190 victims, reported pregnancy in only 0.6 percent." *Dr Stephen Krason*

But, of course, they do come about. Bioethicist Andrew Varga sets out arguments in favor of abortion after rape or incest as follows:

- The mental health of a woman is best safeguarded by abortion.
- As this pregnancy is the result of a grave injustice the victim should not be obliged to carry the fetus to viability.
- A constant reminder about the violence committed against the woman would just increase her mental anguish.
- The value of the woman's mental health is greater than the value of the fetus.
- The fetus is an aggressor against the woman's integrity and personal life and must be repelled even by killing him if that is the only way to defend personal and human values.

Arguments against abortion after rape or incest are summed up as;

The unborn entity can hardly be termed an aggressor when its presence does not endanger its mother's life. It is the rapist who was the aggressor.

Abortion is argued on the grounds of the woman's mental suffering. Against that argument one has to weigh the rightness of homicide of another, being justified to relieve one's emotional distress.

"A child does not lose its right to life simply because its father or its mother was a sexual criminal or a deviant." *Dr. Michael Bauman, theologian and ethicist*

"Psychological studies have shown that, when given the proper support, most pregnant rape victims progressively change their attitudes about their unborn child from something repulsive to someone who is innocent and uniquely worthwhile." *Professor Stephen Krason*

4. Is the unborn baby less than human?

The abortion debate is concerned about the moral status of the unborn. What if the unborn are fully human? Then nearly every abortion performed is tantamount to murder. Many who are termed "pro-choice" campaigners say that although the unborn entity is human, in the sense that it belongs to the *Homo sapiens* species, it is not a person. This leads them to the conclusion that any unborn baby is not fully human.

But, as Ronald Reagon observed, "Abortion is advocated only by persons who have themselves been born."

Some arguments of "pro-choice" adherents

"Pro-choice" campaigners often use one of the two following arguments:

- The decisive moment argument
- The gradualist argument

when they are debating the status of the unborn.

The decisive moment argument

This view agrees that human life does begin at the moment of conception. However, so the argument runs, only at some later stage in the unborn human's development does it deserve to be protected by us. This "moment" is the moment that it becomes a person.

The gradualist argument

The gradualist position argues that the unborn human gradually gains more rights as it develops. For example, a zygote has fewer rights than a 6-month-old fetus. And a 6-month-old fetus has fewer rights than an adult woman.

Pre-natal development

Pregnancy begins at conception, that is, as soon as the male sperm and the female ovum unite. The result, a zygote, is a one-celled biological entity. Every human being was once at this stage of human development.

Many Christians are not happy that this entity is called a "fertilized ovum."

For both ovum and sperm cease to exist at the moment of conception.

There is no question that the zygote is biologically alive. For a zygote fulfills the four criteria needed to establish biological life:

- metabolism
- growth,
- reaction to stimuli
- reproduction (the zygote is capable of cell reproduction and twinning).

Can a zygote be said to be fully human?

1. The zygote is the sexual product of human parents. So what is conceived, the conceptus, is human.
2. The conceptus is a unique human individual, even though it is so tiny.
3. It has its own unique genetic code, consisting of 46 chromosomes, which is neither the mother's nor the father's. No further genetic information is needed to make the unborn entity a unique individual human.

Jermoe L. LeJeune [?Jerome?]

The French geneticist Jermoe L. LeJeune, gave the following testimony before a Senate Subcommittee: "To accept the fact that after fertilization has taken place a new human has come into being is no longer a matter of taste or opinion. The human nature of the human being from conception to old age is not a metaphysical contention, it is plain experimental evidence."

So it is quite reasonable to conclude that the development of a unique individual human life begins at conception.

5. How do "pro-lifers" feel about birth control?

Question:
Surely, people who hold the "pro-life" stance cannot be happy with some forms of artificial birth control?
Answer:
Yes, that is quite right. For some forms of birth control result in the death of the conceptus. This includes forms of birth control such as the IUD and the "morning-after pill". If the pro-life position is right then such birth control is a form of homicide.

But this does not apply to every kind of birth control. Any form of birth control that prevents conception taking place at all, such as use of the condom and sterilization, is okay.

The pro-life advocates like to make a distinction between contraception and birth control.

Contraception and birth control

Contraception literally means "to prevent conception." So all contraception is a form of birth control. For, quite obviously, no birth can take place where there has been no conception.

However, not all forms of birth control are contraceptive, since some forms of birth control prevent birth by killing the conceptus after conception.

Pro-life advocates are not against contraception as a form of family planning.

6. Surely a woman has the right to control her own body?

If a woman has the right to control her own body, is she not entitled to have an abortion?

Arguments against this view

The unborn baby within a pregnant woman's body is not part of her body. The conceptus is a genetically distinct entity, with its own unique and individual gender, blood type, bone-structure and genetic code. While it is true that the unborn baby is attached to its mother, and so totally dependent on the mother, it is not part of her.

A woman does have a right to control her own body. But the unborn baby, though for a time living inside her body, is not part of her body.

So pro-lifers argue that in this situation an abortion is not justified.

6. What is legal?

What is the position concerning abortion and the law in the U.S.?

Roe v. Wade

Many people in America think that the Supreme Court decision *Roe v. Wade*, 1973, only permits abortions up to 24 weeks. It is also widely perceived that after 24 weeks an abortion is only allowed if the pregnant woman's health

is in grave danger. These are false perceptions. The current law does not restrict a woman from having an abortion on practically any grounds, at any time during her pregnancy.

Justice Harry Blackmun

In *Roe v. Wade*, Justice Harry Blackmun divided pregnancy into three trimesters.

First and second three months of pregnancy

He ruled that a state has no right to restrict abortion in the first six months of pregnancy. So a woman could have an abortion during the first two trimesters for any reason she saw fit. There was no distinction made between an unplanned pregnancy, gender selection, convenience or rape.

Last three months of pregnancy

In the last trimester the state has a right, although not an obligation, to restrict abortions to only those cases in which the mother's health is jeopardized.

So *Roe v. Wade* does not prevent a state from allowing unrestricted abortion for the entire nine months of pregnancy if it so chooses.

Nevada and abortion on demand

Like many other states, the state of Nevada has chosen to restrict abortion in the last trimester by only permitting abortions if "there is a substantial risk that the continuance of the pregnancy would endanger the life of the patient or would gravely impair the physical or mental health of the patient."

But in practice this restriction is a restriction in name only.

The Supreme Court so broadly defined "health" in Roe's companion decision, *Doe v. Bolton*, 1973, that for all intents and purposes the current law in every state except Missouri and Pennsylvania allows for abortion on demand.

Defining "health"

In *Bolton* the court ruled that "health" must be taken in its broadest possible medical context, and must be defined "in light of all factors – physical, emotional, psychological, familial and the woman's age – relevant to the well-being of the patient. All these factors relate to health."

The court's health provision has the practical effect of legalizing abortion up until the time of birth, so long as a woman can convince her physician that she needs the abortion to preserve her "emotional health."

Senate Judiciary Committee

So the Senate Judiciary Committee concluded that "no significant legal barriers of any kind whatsoever exist today in the United States for a woman to obtain an abortion for any reason during any stage of her pregnancy."

This runs counter to early Christian teaching in the *Didache* which refers to "child-murderers who slay God's image in the womb."

7. Help, I'm pregnant! Should I go for an abortion?

"I have just found out that I'm pregnant. I'm not married. What should I do?"

The facts

In the USA over one million teenagers will become pregnant this year. On an average that is about 3,000 teenage pregnancies a day. One in nine teenage women will become pregnant this year. Nearly 50% of these teenagers will have an abortion.

No easy answer

There are no easy answers concerning unwanted teenage pregnancies. They cause great pain and anguish. People will be hurt.

What should a counselor say?

1. Even though one mistake has been made, it doesn't mean that you have to keep on making more mistakes.
2. Abortion is not the only option. While an abortion may seem to solve many acute problems, such as temporary embarrassment, it will not solve them all. God hates abortion.

Many teenagers are more than aware that abortion is taking the life of an innocent baby. After all is it not the baby's fault that anyone became pregnant. To kill an innocent child because its mother made a wrong choice is an even worse choice.

Read Psalm 139 to affirm the fact that the Bible clearly teaches that God is actively involved in creating a person even before that person is born.

"For you created my inmost being;
you knit me together in my mothers womb.
I praise you because I am fearfully and wonderfully made; your works are wonderful, I know that full well.
My frame was not hidden from you when I was made in the secret place.
When I was woven together in the depths of the earth,
your eyes saw my unformed body.
All the days ordained for me
were written in your book
before one of them came to be."
Psalm 139:13-16

Not having an abortion

If you decide against abortion, be encouraged that you have done what is right. Also, be encouraged that God has already made good plans for you and your baby. Anyone who tells you how stupid you are for not getting an abortion is wrong. No abortion leaves anyone emotionally untouched.

Should you keep your baby?

This decision should be made after you've weighed up your personal decision. In the light of that decide what would be best for your baby.

Remember God loves you and your unborn baby

God cares for you and your unborn baby. Try reading Psalm 34:17-22.

> "The righteous cry out, and the Lord hears them;
> he delivers them from all their troubles.
> The Lord is close to the brokenhearted and saves those who are crushed in spirit.
> He protects all his bones, not one of them will be broken."

8. What about handicapped children?

Would it not be much better for deformed or handicapped children never to be born?

Down's syndrome

Down's syndrome, previously known as Mongoloidism, which inflicts severe mental retardation, is one reason why babies are killed before birth.

Some, who say that they are looking at the problem from the mother's point of view, argue that abortion should remain a choice for women who do not want to take care of such a child. Some, who say that they are looking at the problem for the handicapped baby's point of view, argue that it is better for such children never to be born rather than to live a life burdened with a serious mental or physical handicap.

Pro-life reply

If the unborn are fully human, then to promote the aborting of the handicapped unborn is no different, morally speaking, from promoting the execution of handicapped people who are already born.

So the question is not whether a handicapped individual is born or unborn, but whether handicapped human life should be protected equally with healthy human life.

"It has been my constant experience that disability and unhappiness do not necessarily go together." *Former U.S. Surgeon General C. Everett Koop, who worked with severely deformed infants as a pediatric surgeon at Philadelphia's Children's Hospital*

Everett Koop has also written: "Some of the most unhappy children whom I have known have all of their physical and mental faculties, and on the other hand some of the happiest youngsters have borne burdens which I myself would find very difficult to bear. Our obligation in such circumstances is to find alternatives for the problems our patients face. I don't consider death an acceptable alternative. With our technology and creativity, we are merely at the beginning of what we can do educationally and in the field of leisure activities for such youngsters. And who knows what happiness is for another person?"

Homicide cannot be justified even if it relieves one of a terrible burden.

A PLEA FROM THREE HANDICAPPED ADULTS

Trowbridge, Kent
8 December, 1962

Sirs:
We were disabled from causes other than Thalidomide, the first of us having two useless arms and hands; the second, two useless legs; and the third, the use of neither arms nor legs.

We were fortunate... in having been allowed to live and we want to say with strong conviction how thankful we are that none took it upon themselves to destroy us as useless cripples.

Here at the Debarue School of spastics, one of the schools of the National Spastic Society, we have found worthwhile and happy lives and we face our future with confidence. Despite our disability, life still has much to offer and we are more than anxious, if only metaphorically, to reach out toward the future.

This, we hope will give comfort and hope to the parents of the Thalidomide babies, and at the same time serve to condemn those who would contemplate the destruction of even a limbless baby.

Yours faithfully,

Elaine Duckett
Glynn Verdon
Caryl Hodges

A plea from three handicapped adults

The following letter appeared in the London *Daily Telegraph,* 8 December 1962, when European newspapers were discussing the use of abortion as an effective means by which to avoid the birth of children who became defective *in utero* due to their mother's use of Thalidomide. This tranquilizer was used by European women in the 1950s and 1960s and caused many children to be born with no arms or legs, or with deformed arms and legs. Thalidomide was never approved by the FDA for sale in the U.S. and was withdrawn in Europe.

There is not a negative correlation between happiness and handicap, as might be assumed.

"Of 200 consecutive suicides at the Baltimore Morgue none had been committed by people with congenital anomalies." *the late Dr Hellegers*

The slippery slope

Will not a society which allows some unborn human beings to forfeit their right to life simply because they have a certain physical deformity or mental handicap soon become a society that will one day view those who have already been born with a similar physical deformity or mental handicap in the same way?

Infant Doe

In 1982, Infant Doe, an Indiana newborn who was born with Down's syndrome and correctable spina bifida, was permitted to die at the request of her parents who asked the attending physician to withhold food and water from the infant.

This parental decision was upheld by an Indiana court. Since her spina bifida was correctable by surgery, if Infant Doe had not been "retarded," her parents would have requested the necessary surgery.

So spina bifida did not kill Infant Doe. Her parents neglected her simply because she had Down's syndrome.

A Down's syndrome citizen

At the time of the death of Infant Doe, the columnist George Will wrote about his own son, Jonathan, a Down's syndrome citizen:

"When a commentator has a direct personal interest in an issue, it behoves him to say so. Some of my best friends are Down's syndrome citizens. (Citizens are what Down's syndrome children are if they avoid being homicide victims in hospitals.)

Jonathan Will, 10, fourth-grader and Orioles fan, has Down's syndrome. He does not "suffer from" Down's syndrome. He suffers from nothing, except anxiety about the Orioles' lousy start. He is doing nicely, thank you. But he is bound to have quite enough problems dealing with society – receiving rights, let alone

empathy. He can do without people like Infant Doe's parents, and courts like Indiana's asserting by their actions the principle that people like him are less than fully human. On the evidence, Down's syndrome citizens have little to learn about being human from people responsible for the death of Infant Doe."

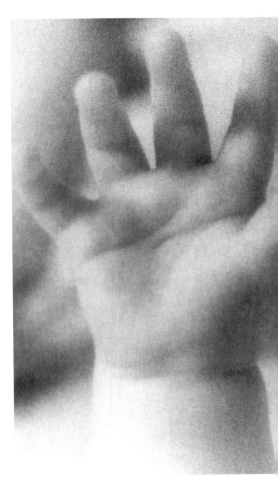

Raising children

General Christian principles

1. A word to fathers

- "Fathers, do not exasperate your children; instead, bring them up in the training and instruction of the Lord." *Ephesians 6:4*
- "Fathers, do not embitter your children, or they will become discouraged." *Colossians 3:21*

Nobody likes a heavy-handed father.

2. A word to mothers

- "I have been reminded of your sincere faith, which first lived in your grandmother Lois and in your mother Eunice and, I am persuaded, now lives in you also." *2 Timothy 1:5*
- The greatest gift any parent or grandparent can give to their children or grandchildren is the example of their own "sincere faith" in God.

3. A word to children

- "Children, obey your parents in the Lord, for this is right. 'Honor your father and mother...that it may go well with you.'" *Ephesians 6:1-3*
- "A wise son heeds his father's instruction, but a mocker does not listen to rebuke." *Proverbs 13:1*

IF A CHILD LIVES WITH...

If a child lives with criticism,
    he learns to condemn.
If a child lives with hostility,
    he learns to fight.
If a child lives with fear,
    he learns to be apprehensive.
If a child lives with pity,
    he learns to feel sorry for himself.
If a child lives with jealousy,
    he learns to feel guilty.
If a child lives with encouragement,
    he learns to be self-confident.
If a child lives with tolerance,
    he learns to be patient.
If a child lives with praise,
    he learns to be appreciative.
If a child lives with acceptance,
    he learns to love.
If a child lives with approval,
    he learns to like himself.
If a child lives with recognition,
    he learns to have a goal.
If a child lives with fairness,
    he learns what justice is.
If a child lives with honesty,
    he learns what truth is.
If a child lives with sincerity,
    he learns to have faith in himself
    and those around him.
If a child lives with love,
    he learns that the world is
    a wonderful place to live in.

Author unknown

Moral choices

Every day parents make scores of moral decisions in the context of their own families:

Bullying at school: should we tell our children to give as good as they get? Should we report the bully to the school? Should be do nothing?

In-laws and grandparents: How are we to tell them that we want to have a holiday on our own, just with the kids? Are we being unkind to do this? Do we need more time on our own as a family? Whatever we decide it seems that somebody will be put out.

Shouting at the kids: If we don't they never get up in the morning. But does this mean that they will shout at their own kids? Do I want that to happen?

TV, videos and the Internet: Should we just let them watch everything they find? Should we create parental controls on the Internet and set up specific levels of access for each screen name (child)? Should we teach our children not to watch "nasty bits" in films, such as gratuitous violence? Should we tell our children not to watch any nasty videos that might be shown in the homes of their friends?

AN IMMORAL ACT

"Give up money, give up fame, give up science, give up the earth itself, and all it contains, rather than do an immoral act.' *Thomas Jefferson*

'When You Thought I Wasn't Looking'

When you thought I wasn't looking,
 I saw you hang my first painting on
 the refrigerator, and I wanted to
 paint another one.
When you thought I wasn't looking,
 I saw you feed a stray cat, and I
 thought it was good to be kind to
 animals.
When you thought I wasn't looking,
 I saw you make my favorite cake for
 me, and I knew that little things are
 special things.
When you thought I wasn't looking, I
 heard you pray, and I believed there
 is a God I could always talk to.
When you thought I wasn't looking,
 I felt you kiss me goodnight, and I
 felt loved.
When you thought I wasn't looking,
 I saw tears come from your eyes,
 and I learned that sometimes things
 hurt, but it's all right to cry.
When you thought I wasn't looking,
 I saw you give to someone needy
 and I learned the joy of giving.
When you thought I wasn't looking,
 I saw you always did your best
 and it made me want to be all that
 I could be.
When you thought I wasn't looking,
 I heard you say "thank you" and I
 wanted to say thanks for all the
 things I saw when you thought I
 wasn't looking. *Author unknown*

No list of dos and don'ts

We have the Ten Commandments and
all the moral teaching in the Bible as our
guide. But this does not mean to say that
we have the perfect answer to every
problem that arises. Christians may
bring up their children in a variety of
different ways. It's not as if we have a
checklist of dos and don'ts that we refer
to each day. Rather, there are overriding
Christian principles, such as: love;
attempting to live in a way that Jesus
would have done or would have
approved of; naturally turning to prayer
in difficult times, as well as in happy
times.

It is such principles that Christian
parents, consciously or unconsciously,
should attempt to bring to bear on every
family crisis as well as the endless every
day problems.

Thoughts of C. S. Lewis

"If no set of moral ideas were truer or
better than any other, there would be
no reason in preferring civilized to
savage morality or Christian morality
to Nazi morality."

"The moment you say that one set of
moral ideas can be better than
another, you are, in fact, measuring
them both by a standard, saying that
one of them conforms to that standard
more nearly than the other."

3   PERSONAL LIFESTYLE

CONTENTS

Introduction

Jesus

Jesus emphasized that his teaching, and not the ideas of human teachers, should be the yardstick for measuring conduct. For example, Jesus once said, "You have heard that it was said, 'Love your neighbor and hate your enemy'" (Matthew 5:43). At first glance this appears to be a quotation from the Old Testament. But you can search from Genesis to Malachi for the quotation without finding it. Jesus was actually quoting the accepted teaching of the rabbis, and was saying, in effect, that the traditional religious teaching was wrong. He then went on to talk about turning the other cheek and going the extra mile. Jesus' moral teaching, far from being chained to his own day as some people suggest, was vastly superior to it.

Paul and 1 Corinthians

Far from having nothing to say about moral issues, the New Testament is full of such teaching. Nearly all of the letters of the apostle Paul start with a section of doctrinal teaching, and then move on to very down-to-earth teaching about moral issues.

Take Paul's first letter to a group of new Christians who lived in Corinth, a city that was a byword for immorality. In 1 Corinthians Paul gives moral teaching on urgent moral issues that were upsetting the church:

- Is it acceptable for a man to sleep with his step-mother? 5:1-13.

- May a Christian take a fellow Christian to court? 6:1-8.
- Christians are free, aren't they? So aren't they free to have illicit sex? 6:12-20.
- Are Christians free to marry, to divorce, to remarry after a divorce, to seek a divorce if married to an unbeliever, to marry again after the death of a first partner? 7:1-40.
- Is it wrong to eat food that has been offered to idols? 8:1-13.

Overall principle

All our individual actions have social implications. When it comes to considering our own personal lifestyle and the impact it has on other Christians one of the most important biblical principles to apply to ourselves is that we should do nothing that will cause a fellow Christian to stumble. See 1 Corinthians 8:11-13.

Drinking alcohol

Some background facts and figures

Would some Christians who take the line, "The Bible condemns drunkenness but not drinking" change and say, "People would be better off if they did not drink at all" if they knew the following facts?

- Alcohol is America's number one drug.
- Alcohol is the third leading cause of death.
- 50-60% of the children of alcoholics will become alcoholics.
- 76% of the children who parents are total abstainers, themselves become total abstainers
- 50% of murders involve alcohol.
- 33% of all suicides involve alcohol.
- 60% of child abuse involves alcohol.
- 50% of all auto fatalities involve alcohol.
- Fewer American Soldiers died during the Vietnam Conflict than die each year as a result of alcohol use.
- Alcohol is the number one cause of death for teens.
- Alcohol-related expenses are four times greater than the tax revenue generated by alcohol.
- Every twentieth alcoholic is a pre-teen.
- Alcoholics outnumber drug addicts 10 to 1.
- According to Harvard nutritionist Jean Mayer the grain used in distilling alcohol would feed 20 million starving people each year.

- According to the Health and Human Services Department of the National Institute on Alcohol Abuse and Alcoholism our annual alcohol-related expenses total $68,617,579,000.00 per year.

Drunkenness

The Bible is against people getting drunk.

Underestimating the evils of drunkenness

Some Christians who are total abstainers from strongly held convictions feel that some of their fellow-Christians who are not total abstainers may not have given sufficient heed to the undoubted strong warnings in the Bible against drunkenness.

- Noah got drunk after the flood: Genesis 9:21.
- Warnings from the book of Proverbs: Proverbs 23:19-21.
- The prophet Isaiah often spoke out against drunkenness: Isaiah 5:11, 12; 22:12, 13; 24:9-12; 28:1; 56:10-12. "And these also stagger from wine and reel from beer: Priests and prophets stagger from beer and are befuddled with wine; they reel from beer, they stagger when seeing visions, they stumble when rendering decisions." Isaiah 28:7
- Paul writes, "Let us behave decently, as in the daytime, not in orgies and drunkenness" Romans 13.

It is sad to think that a number of the above warnings were not directed towards ungodly people, but to God's people who lived in a state of drunkenness. Some of the Christians at Corinth even turned up drunk when they came to the Lord's supper, 1 Corinthians 11:21. See also: Ephesians 5:18; 1 Thessalonians 5:6-8; 1 Timothy 3:2, 3; Titus 1:7, 8; 1 Peter 1:13; 4:2.

Should all Christians be total abstainers?

Some Christians are total abstainers just because they've never been fond of drinking.

Other Christians are total abstainers and have very strong convictions on the subject and feel certain that this is right for them.

Some Christians would go so far as to say that all Christians should be total abstainers.

Some Christians believe that to have an alcoholic drink in public is a bad witness.

Some Christians also know that, for them, social drinking might or would lead them into becoming seriously addicted to alcohol, and so are total abstainers.

Don't condemn your fellow-Christian

It is not the business of a Christian who is not a total abstainer to pass judgment on a Christian who is a total abstainer.

"The man who eats everything must not look down on him who does not,

and the man who does not eat everything must not condemn the man who does, for God has accepted him." *Romans 14:3*

What Bible principles guide us here?

1. Be convinced

"Each one should be fully convinced in his own mind" *Romans 14:5.*

2. Live for the Lord and give thanks to God, whether you are total abstainer or not

"He who eats meat, eats to the Lord, for he gives thanks to God; and he who abstains, does so to the Lord and gives thanks to God." *Romans 14:6*

The Bible and alcohol

It is easy to show that the Bible is against drunkenness. But that is not the total picture.

1. A gift from God

For, in itself, there is nothing wrong with wine. Indeed, it is a gift from God. "Wine," says the psalmist, "gladdens the heart of man" Psalm 104:15.

The clear teaching of the Bible is that wine is a gift from God. This in itself does not mean that everyone has to go ahead and drink it. So it is unnecessary to justify drinking alcohol by saying that Jesus made water into wine at Cana, John 2:1-11, or that because Paul told Timothy to drink some sine for medicinal purposes, we should therefore drink wine.

2. Jesus was not a total abstainer

Clearly Jesus was not a total abstainer, for he was, wrongly, accused of being a drunkard. "For John [the Baptist] came neither eating nor drinking, and they say, 'He has a demon.' The Son of Man came eating and drinking, and they say, 'Here is a glutton and a drunkard, a friend of tax collectors and "sinners".' But wisdom is proved right by her actions." *Matthew 11:18, 19*

But just because Jesus was not a total abstainer, that in itself does not mean to say that we must all drink alcohol. It is also clear from this that some people, like John the Baptist, feel that it is definitely right for them to be a total abstainer.

To abstain or not to abstain?

ABSTINENCE OR MODERATION?
"Total abstinence is easier than perfect moderation."
Augustine of Hippo

ABSTINENCE AND CHARITY
"Abstinence without charity is useless."
Gildas

PURITANS AND ABSTINENCE
"Puritans were the opposite of those who bear that name today: as young, fierce, progressive intellectuals, very fashionable and up-to-date, they were not teetotallers."
C. S. Lewis

ABSTINENCE AND HOLINESS
"Abstinence by itself is not holiness, but if it be discreet it helps us to be holy."
Richard Rolle

A FALSE ARGUMENT
"An individual Christian may see fit to give up all sorts of things for special reasons – marriage, or meat, or beer, or cinema; but the moment he starts saying the things are bad in themselves, or looking down his nose at other people who do use them, he has taken the wrong turning."
C. S. Lewis

ANOTHER FALSE ARGUMENT
"If you say, 'Would there were no wine' because of the drunkards; then you must say, if you use that argument, 'Would there were no steel,' because of the murderers; 'Would there were no night,' because of the thieves; 'Would there were no light,' because of the informers; and 'Would there were no women,' because of adultery."
John Chrysostom

RECEIVE WITH THANKSGIVING
"For everything God created is good, and nothing is to be rejected if it is received with thanksgiving, because it is consecrated by the word of God and prayer."
1 Timothy 4:4, 5

Warnings against becoming drunk

WINE MOCKS

"Wine is a mocker, strong drink is raging."

Proverbs 20:1, KJV

GAZING AT WINE

"Do not gaze at wine when it is red, when it sparkles in the cup, when it goes down smoothly! In the end it bites like a snake and poisons like a viper."

Proverbs 23:31, 32

DO NOT GET DRUNK

"Do not get drunk on wine, which leads to debauchery. Instead, be filled with the Spirit."

Ephesians 5:18

THE DEVIL'S BACK DOOR

"Drunkenness is the devil's back door to hell and everything that hellish. For he that once gives away his brains to drink is ready to be caught by Satan for anything."

C. H. Spurgeon

YOU DON'T NEED TO BE TOTAL ABSTAINER TO BE AGAINST DRUNKENNESS

"My soul might be perpetually dropping showers of tears, if it might know the doom and destruction brought on by that one demon, and by that one demon only! Though I am no total abstainer, I hate drunkenness as much as any man breathing, and have been the means of bringing many poor creatures to relinquish this bestial indulgence. We believe drunkenness to be an awful crime and a horrid sin. We stand prepared to go to war with it. How many thousands are murdered every year by that accursed devil of drunkenness!"

C. H. Spurgeon

ADVISE OF AN UNBELIEVER

"Drunkenness is temporary suicide: the happiness that it brings is merely negative, a momentary cessation of unhappiness."

Bertrand Russell

A BEAST

"While the wine is in thy hand, thou art a man; when it is in thine head, thou art become a beast."

Thomas Adam

Living and dying to the Lord

There is no reason for Christians to quarrel if they come to different conclusions about this matter. For we know that "none of us lives to himself alone and none of us dies to himself alone. If we live, we live to the Lord; and if we die, we die to the Lord. So, whether we live or die, we belong to the Lord" Romans 14:7.

Drug abuse and smoking

Drug abuse

Drugs are often freely available at certain places, such as raves and discos, and so Christians should avoid such places.

Drugs and the World Health Organization

The WHO dossier lists five main consequences of drug abuse:

- Economic losses affecting the user, his social circle and his society.
- Deteriorating family relationships, failure in user's role as parent/marriage partner.
- Increasing likelihood of involvement in criminal behavior (to finance the addiction), road accidents, mishaps at work, drug trafficking and offenses committed while under the influence of drugs.
- Increased demand for social service, health care, legal aid.
- Friends and contacts influenced to take drugs also.

Health problems that arise among drug users include:

- Injuries incurred while driving etc. under the influence of drugs
- Infections such as scrum hepatitis and septicemia from use of syringes.
- Death (accidental or intentional) from overdosing or using a mixture of drugs.
- Sickness resulting from neglect of personal hygiene.
- Malnutrition, nutritional deficiencies.

- Toxic psychoses (may be precipitated by a single dose).
- Tissue damage (also occurs in fetus if pregnant woman overuses alcohol, tobacco etc.).

Smoking

On the grounds that smoking and drug abuse are addictive and bad for our health it seems that no Christian would ever want to indulge in such activities.

Paul reminds us that we are temples of God's Holy Spirit, who is in us and who we have received from God, 1 Corinthians 6:19. "You are not your own; you were bought with a price. Therefore honor God with you body." *1 Corinthians 6:20*

Many people became addicted to smoking before they became Christians. Some smokers kick the habit on becoming Christians, but not all manage to give up smoking. It is not up to non-smoking Christians to condemn them. Smokers themselves are usually the first people to say that they wished that they had never started in the first place.

Gambling

Defining gambling

Gambling has been defined as risking what is yours to get what belongs to someone else without any service being given or any merchandise exchanged.

The many forms of gambling

- card games
- dice
- numbers
- betting on elections
- buying sweepstakes tickets
- betting on horse races
- slot machines
- betting on sporting events
- various types of sports pools
- bingo
- buying tickets in raffles
- betting on recreational activities
- lotteries

Taking risks and gambling

There is a great deal of difference between gambling and the risks we take every day.

Gambling is different in that it involves the creation of unnecessary risks, which may endanger one's finances. The creation of these risks undermines, and may destroy, such Christian virtues as productive work, thrift and the desire to earn what one claims the right to have. Gambling is sinful because it involves the desire to obtain something for nothing.

Bible principles and gambling

1. Stewardship

- God made the earth and everything in it, Psalm 24:1.
- Christians are meant to be good stewards of God's gifts, see 1 Peter 4:10.
- Jesus taught that we will have to give an account of our stewardship, Luke 16:1, 2.
- Paul taught that we should be faithful stewards, 1 Corinthians 4:2.

This stands in stark contrast with wasting and gambling away what has been entrusted to us by God.

2. Work

Paul taught that those who do not work should not eat, 1 Thessalonians 3:10. The philosophy that embraces the "something for nothing" attitude violates the work principle given by God.

3. Becoming enslaved

Gambling often turns into an addiction, which it is often seemingly impossible to kick. Contrast with this the attitude the apostle Paul applied to himself in 1 Corinthians 9:27.

4. Covetousness

The reason for gambling is often a form of covetousness. See Ephesians 5:5; Proverbs 1:19; 21:25, 26; 23:4, 5; 30:8, 9.

5. The danger of materialism

Materialism characterizes our society today and it is all too easy for Christians to become enmeshed in one of its many forms. Hence there are strong warnings in the Bible against a materialistic and acquisitive attitude in life. See Matthew 19:23, 24; 1 Timothy 6:5-11.

"Put to death, therefore, whatever belongs to your earthly nature:...evil desires and greed." Colossians 3:5.

How can a little flutter do any harm?

One things leads to another. There is no point in starting to engage in any form of gambling. Indeed it can be very dangerous for it may give you a taste for gambling. A person who is today addicted to gambling started his habit is some tiny and seemingly harmless bet.

Buying a ticket for a good cause

Everyone in the office is being asked to buy a ticked for a good cause and the first prize for the lucky winner will be a brand new car.

Now what is the Christian to do? If he refuses to buy a ticket he looks stingy and appears not to want to support a good cause. If the cause really is a good cause and worthy of support then a Christian might buy a ticket, but not give his name and address. This will take away the element of gambling from donating something to a good cause.

Paying taxes

Paying taxes

There is no getting round Romans 13:6, 7: "This is also why you pay taxes…Give everyone what you owe him: if you owe taxes, pay taxes." Christians are told that they should pay their taxes.

Accountants

If a Christian employs the sharpest accountant in town who specializes in tax law he may reduce his tax bill and not cross the line into tax evasion. He may break no state law but he may not be keeping the spirit of Romans 13:6, 7.

"This is why you pay taxes, for the authorities are God's servants, who give their full time to governing. Give everyone what you owe him: If you owe taxes, pay taxes; if reverence then reverence…"

What's so wrong about tax evasion?

"Everybody does it, so why shouldn't Christians? It's only like telling a white lie, isn't it?" What goes by the name of "tax evasion" should go by the name of "stealing."

High standards

It is much easier for Christians to adopt the standards of the world than high moral standards, which are based on Christian principles. We all deplore looting and stealing, but we may secretly admire somebody who gets away with not paying all of his taxes.

Christians are not meant to steal

"He who has been stealing must steal no more." *Ephesians 4:28*

Liars are grouped with murderers

To fill in a tax form in a dishonest way is to tell a lie.

"We know that the law is good if one uses it properly. We also know that law is made not for the righteous but for lawbreakers and rebels, the ungodly and sinful; the unholy and irreligious; for those who kill their fathers and mothers, for murderers, for adulterers and perverts, for slave traders and *liars*…"
1 Timothy 1:8-10.

What is the occult, magick and Satanism?

1. The Christian and the occult

Is it necessary, or even wise, for Christians to know about the occult? In a word, the Bible teaching on the occult is that we should not touch it with a barge-pole.

For many Christians it is not necessary to go into all the ins and outs of the occult. If you are in any doubt about learning about the occult, stay clear of such information. Don't even read the following pages! But it may be helpful for some Christians to be able to identify some of the more common manifestations of the evils of the occult so that they themselves, as well as others, can steer clear.

We are not to be immersed in evil. But what about such things as horoscopes, Ouija boards, Halloween? Are they not just a bit of harmless fun? Should Christians appear to be killjoys and speak against them?

Innocent and shrewd

We are not meant to be gullible or naive. Jesus told his disciples, "be as shrewd as snakes and as innocent as doves" Matthew 10:16.

2. WHAT IS A CULT?

Don't some Christians come down rather hard on cults?

Some cults are full of evil and it is the duty of Christians to prevent anyone, especially young people who may be impressionable and gullible, from joining them.

A cult is an evil belief system. Cults nearly always have an authoritarian leader who most often claims to have special powers with secret or esoteric capabilities and knowledge.

Many cults, such as the Charles Manson Cult, the Peoples Temple Cult, the AUM- Shinrikyo have been linked with Satanism and mass murders or "suicides."

3. What is the occult?

The word "occult" means hidden, concealment or the unknown. Examples of occultism are magick, paganism, witchcraft and Satanism.

Two characteristics of the occult

  a. Everything is thought to be energy. Magic manipulates and alters energy through one's will, the use of rituals and incantations.
  b. There is no absolute reality, truth or morality. Truth is found through subjective experience.

4. What is Magick?

Magic and magick

The term "magick" is often spelled by occultists with a "k" to distinguish it from stage magic.

Magick is an occult art. It has been described as "a pseudo-science designed to manipulate one's environment, to communicate with and control nonphysical forces or supernatural powers through one's will." These powers are called

- spirit forces
- spirit beings
- familiar spirits
- spirit guides
- spirit helpers
- deceiving spirits
- guardian spirits
- demons.

Magick is an essential ritual tool used in:

- ancestor worship
- animism
- paganism
- satanism
- sorcery
- voodoo
- witchcraft (wicca).

5. What is Satanism?

Satanism is a secret religion, which incorporates an alliance and worshipful allegiance to the Devil and his cause. Through direct worship of this evil angel, the Satanist seeks to obtain a pre-hell power through selected sorcery teachings and magickal rituals.

"Satan promises the best, but pays with the worst; he promises honor, and pays with disgrace; he promises pleasure, and pays with pain; he promises profit, and pays with loss; he promises life, and pays with death. But God pays as he promises; all his payments are made in pure gold."
Thomas Brooks

What about witchcraft?

What is witchcraft?

Witchcraft is the occult art of attempting to willfully shape one's environment through the mediumistic summoning of forbidden supernatural power.

The witch or wiccan seeks to harness magickal powers behind various belief systems such as:

- animism
- nature religions
- magickal fantasy religions
- feminist spirituality
- mythologies
- mysticism
- pantheism
- fertility rituals
- ceremonial magick
- polytheism.

Contemporary witchcraft is not Satanism. Witchcraft is another spiritual facet of neo-paganism.

Black magic and white magic

Witches claim that sorcery is black magic used for evil, but that they practice white magic, magic for good.

Christian reply:

The Bible knows of no distinction between "good" and "bad" magic or sorcery. All sorcery has the same Satanic source. All sorcery is hated by God.

The Bible's advice

"See to it that no one makes a prey of you by philosophy and empty deceit, according to human tradition, according to the elemental spirits of the universe, and not according to Christ."
Colossians 2:8

The overriding principle

The Bible warns believers to "abstain from every form of evil" 1 Thessalonians 5:22. The Old and the New Testaments give strong warnings about avoiding evil practices:

"Do not practice divination or sorcery."
Leviticus 19:26

"The acts of the sinful nature are obvious:...idolatry and witchcraft..."
Galatians 5:19, 20

In many places in the Bible we read about God's severe judgments on anything associated with sorcery. See Isaiah 47:9; Jeremiah 14:14; 27:9; Malachi 3:5; Revelation 9:21; 18:23; 21:8; 22:15.

Judgment

"But the beast was captured, and with him the false prophet who had performed the miraculous signs on his behalf. With these signs he had deluded those who had received the mark of the beast and worshiped his image. The two of them were thrown alive into the fiery lake of burning sulfur." *Revelation 19:21*

Know your Bible

Helpful verses about divination, sorcery and magic are:

- Exodus 22:18
- Leviticus 19:26, 31; 20:6, 27
- Deuteronomy 18:10-12
- 1 Samuel 15:23

- 2 Kings 17:17; 23:24
- 1 Chronicles 10:13
- Isaiah 2:6; 8:19, 20; 47:12-15
- Ezekiel 13:20-23
- Daniel 2:27, 28; 5:15-17
- Acts 7: 41-44; 13:7-10; 16:16-18
- Galatians 5:19, 20.

What about spirit contact?

Spirit contact: who is on the other side?

It seems that an increasing number of people who have lost loved ones want to find out if they are not at peace. Many people want to seek advice from a departed loved one.

What is spirit contact?

Spirit contact is the attempt to contact a disembodied being. Such a being might be a dead person, or an angel, or a spirit guide or a demon.

Spiritualism is alive and well in the United States. It teaches that one can and should contact departed souls for advice.

Differing types of spirit contact

Mediums, channelers, and psychics all go in for (supposedly) contacting spirits.

Mediums claim to contact dead spirits of people by allowing the spirit to speak through them or by passing on messages from the spirits.

Seances

Seances comprise a group of people who meet to contact the spirit of a departed loved one of someone present.

Channelers

Channelers claim to contact spirit beings other than the dead, such as angels, aliens or so-called advanced spiritual beings.

They may do this by allowing the spirit to speak through them. For example, J. Z. Knight claims to channel

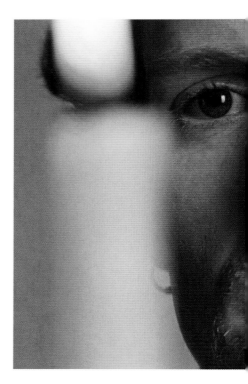

Ramptha, who claims to be a 35,000-year-old warrior.

It is worth noting that the messages from the "dead," from the spirits, and from channeled entities never encourage people to believe in Jesus or in the truths of the Bible!

What does God say about spirit contact?

Deuteronomy 18:10-12 forbids:

- divination
- sorcery
- spirit contact
- consulting mediums

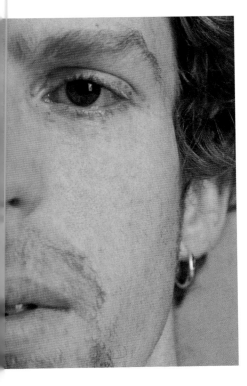

One puts oneself in a vulnerable position by using the Board. One is not merely "playing" this "game," one is showing an interest in spirit contact.

If contact is made, it is demons, evil spirits or fallen angels, and not the dead, who are responding. If Satan is able to disguise himself as "an angel of light" 2 Corinthians 11:14, then it is not difficult for fallen angels to disguise themselves as the dead.

Just because the Ouija Board is marketed as a game that does not mean to say that it is harmless.

Occult attempts to contact spirit beings; spiritism

These spirit beings include fallen angels, demons, departed souls, or those believed to be in other planes or dimensions. This activity uses:

- Ouija Boards
- channeling
- meditation
- visualization
- drugs
- automatic writing.

- consulting those who contact the dead
- casting spells
- heeding omens.

What about the Ouija Board?

The name "Ouija" is a combination of the French and German words for "yes": "Oui" and "Ja." The main purpose of the board is to contact disembodied spirits.

Contacting the dead, necromancy, and contacting spirits, spiritism, are both condemned by God. See Deuteronomy 18:9-12; Leviticus 19:31; 20:6; 1 Samuel 28; 2 Kings 21:6; Isaiah 8:19; 19:3, 4.

"When men tell you to consult mediums and spiritists, who whisper and mutter, should not a people enquire of their God? Why consult the dead on behalf of the living? To the law and to the testimony! If they do not speak according this word, they have no light of dawn." *Isaiah 8:19*

Astrology and horoscopes

What is astrology?

Astrology is more than the horoscope columns in the newspapers and in magazines. Astrology is an occult practice, rooted in ancient Babylon.

Astrology is the belief that the planets, sun and moon are external and internal signposts for individuals or society to follow in order to understand themselves and choose the best options.

It is thought that a person's birth time and place happen at a particular time when the planetary configurations will reveal that person's character and path in this life. A chart of the planetary positions is cast by the astrologer which involves mathematical formulas for determining the planetary positions at a certain moment and place.

The astrologer interprets the chart according to the meanings signified by the planets, sun and moon, the significance of the houses, the meaning of the zodiac signs, and how the planets relate to each other.

Astrology and the Bible

- Astrology cannot be combined with Christian belief in any way.
- Astrology is condemned explicitly in the Bible, Isaiah 47:13-14.
- Astrology is condemned in passages that condemn divination and worshiping the heavens. (See Deuteronomy 4:19; 17:3; 18:9-12; 2 Kings 17:16; Jeremiah 10:2; Acts 7:42.)
- God would hardly give anyone a "gift" for doing something he so clearly condemns.
- By attributing special meaning to planetary positions, one is honoring these celestial bodies. At the same time one is rejecting God's commands about seeking his advice, Isaiah 8:19, 20; Daniel 2:27, 28.

What about horoscopes?

Horoscope columns in many daily newspapers and magazines are written by people who believe in astrology, and have a world-view at odds with God's Word. They may appear to give helpful advice. Most people regard them as harmless fun. But see 2 Corinthians 11:14, 15.

Horoscope columns are fruits of the occult. For many they become addictive reading. Consulting horoscopes boils down to honoring an occult practice

"...Satan himself masquerades as an angel of light. It is not surprising, then, if his servants masquerade as servants of righteousness."

Halloween

Need Christians be concerned with Halloween?
Its origin

The origins of Halloween can be traced back to Celtic and pagan rituals. People then believed that Samhain, the Celtic name for Halloween, pronounced "sow-ain", was a time when the veil between this world and the next was thinnest. This meant that communication and contact with spirits or the spiritual realm was at its strongest.

Samhain celebrates the beginning of winter, marked by death, and the beginning of the Celtic New Year.

Christian response

Christians should not live in fear or dread of this day. But we should be aware that witches and Satanists mark this day as one of their eight sacred or special days of celebration.

Trick-or-treat

Some Christians think of this as a piece of harmless fun. Others ban their children from taking part in it and do not allow their children to dress up as a witch, demon, devil, ghost or any other figure that belongs to the world of death or the occult.

Churches often lay on alternative celebrations, such as a harvest celebration.

Bible teaching about the occult and the paranormal

1. Satan disguises himself as someone good
See 2 Corinthians 11:13-15

2. Do not link up or even associate with evil
"Have nothing to do with the fruitless deeds of darkness, but rather expose them." *Ephesians 5:11*

3. God is against sorcery, divination and spirit contact
See Deuteronomy 18:10-12.

4. Christians should consult God, not psychics or channelers
See Isaiah 8:19, 20

5. God is against astrology
"Let your astrologers come forward, those stargazers who make predictions month by month, let them save you from what is to come upon you. Surely they are like stubble; the fire will burn them up. They cannot even save themselves from the power of the flame." *Isaiah 47:13, 14*

6. The occult tries to turn us away from truth
"The proconsul, an intelligent man, sent for Barnabas and Saul because he wanted to hear the word of God. But Elymas the sorcerer...opposed them and tried to turn the proconsul from he faith. Then Saul, who was also called Paul, filled with the Holy Spirit, looked straight at Elymas and said, 'You are a

child of the devil and an enemy of everything that is right!'" *Acts 13:7-10*

7. Be on the alert for Satan and his activities
Satan is always on the prowl: "Be self-controlled and alert. Your enemy the devil prowls around like a roaring lion looking for someone to devour." *1 Peter 5:8*

8. The way to resist Satan
"Submit yourselves, then, to God. Resist the devil, and he will flee from you." *James 4:7*

9. We are kept safe in Jesus
"The one who is in you is greater than the one who is in the world." *1 John 4:4*

Over-eating

Physical appetites

God made us in a way that we take pleasure in quenching our thirst and satisfying our hunger.

It is God who "richly provides us with everything for our enjoyment" 1 Timothy 6:17.

Not only does God give us good gifts to enjoy, Paul reminds the Corinthians that everything should be done to God's glory: "So whether you eat or drink or whatever you do, do it all for the glory of God." *1 Corinthians 10:31*

Warnings

However there are numerous warnings about over-eating in the Bible.

"Do not join those who drink too much wine or gorge themselves on meat, for drunkards and gluttons become poor."
Proverbs 23: 20, 21

"If you find honey, eat just enough – too much of it, and you will vomit."
Proverbs 25:16

Exercise

When the apostle Paul compared physical exercise with godliness he said, "physical training is of some value, but godliness has value for all things holding promise for...the life to come" 1 Timothy 4:8. Paul is not writing off physical exercise, for he says that it does have "some value."

Does gluttony matter?

The Proverbs says, "a greedy man brings trouble to his family" Proverbs 15:27.

Moderation

The way to defeat gluttony is by self-discipline and moderation.

"Eat and drink with moderation and thankfulness for health, not for unprofitable pleasure. Never please your appetite in food or drink when it is prone to be detrimental to your health. Remember the sin of Sodom: 'Look, this was the iniquity of your sister Sodom: She and her daughter had pride, fullness of food and abundance of idleness' Ezekiel 16:49 KJV. The Apostle Paul wept when he mentioned those 'whose end is destruction, whose god is their belly, and whose glory is in their shame – who set their minds on earthly things, being enemies to the cross of Christ' Philippians 3:18, 19 KJV. O then 'do not live according to the flesh lest you die'
Romans 8:13." *Richard Baxter*

Gluttons galore

"Mankind, since the improvements of cookery, eats twice as much as nature requires." *Benjamin Franklin*

Stewardship

Not just giving money

The biblical idea of stewardship includes a wide variety of things, such as caring for the planet earth, and the wise use of our time and talents. Stewardship does not just refer to giving money.

This makes us ask such questions as: "Have I got my priorities right when it comes to the amount of time I give to my family, my work, my local Christian fellowship?"

Giving money

When it comes to giving money to the Lord's work it is easy to establish certain principles from the Bible. Giving money should be done

- regularly
- in proportion to one's income
- with a cheerful heart.

See 1 Corinthians 16:2; 2 Corinthians 9:7.

How much?

These principles give us general guidance about giving money but we are still left with certain questions.

1. How much should I give?

In the Old Testament a tithe, that is 10%, is recommended. But there is no precise figure mentioned in the New Testament. Some Christians believe that this means that 10% is therefore a minimum, and now that we live under the new covenant we should gladly give more.

2. Before or after tax?

If I were to give 10% of my income does this mean 10% of my take home pay, or 10% of my gross income? This raises difficult problems. What if I gave 10% of my gross pay and so did not have enough money left to send my children to college? If I were a single person it would be easy to give 10% of my gross income, but it's different for a married

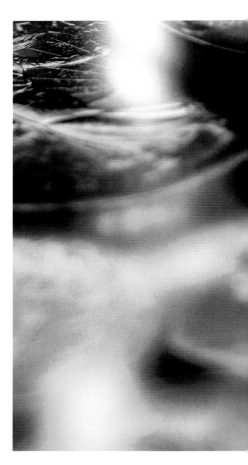

person with heavy family commitments. And what proportion should I give if I am retired and have to live on a small pension?

To whom – local or global?

Then there is the question about to whom I should give money. Should it be all to my local Christian fellowship, as they support some overseas

missionary work, or should I give some money to my local fellowship and some money to missionary societies and agencies engaged in famine relief?

John Wesley

When John Wesley's income increased he did not spend more money on himself and on his family, but he just kept the same amount of money that he had always done, and then gave away all of the rest.

Providing for the future

Our whole society is geared to providing for ourselves financially for the future. Indeed the *KJV* reading of 1 Timothy 5:8 calls people who do not look after their own families financially, "worse that pagans." "If anyone does not provide for his relatives, and especially for his immediate family, he has denied the faith and is worse than an unbeliever."

More from John Wesley

"Any Christian who takes for himself anything more than the plain necessities of life lives in an open, habitual denial of the Lord."
John Wesley

Wesley summed up his attitude to money in the following way:
"Get all you can,
save all you can,
and give all you can."

Suicide: is it an option for a Christian?

Suicides in the Bible

There are six suicides recorded in the Bible:

- Samson's: Judges 16:30
- Saul's: 1 Samuel 31:4
- Saul's armor-bearer: 1 Samuel 31:5
- Ahithophel's, who hanged himself: 2 Samuel 17:23
- Zimri's: 1 Kings 16:18
- Judas Iscariot's: Matthew 27:5.

Depression and suicide

Christians are not exempt from illness. In the past, a number of godly people have felt so depressed that they have contemplated killing themselves.

Job in his suffering cursed the day he

was born. "After this, Job opened his mouth and cursed the day of his birth. He said: 'May the day of my birth perish, and the night it was said, "A boy is born!"'" *Job 3:1-3*

Elijah in his exhaustion and depression asked for his life to be taken away. "He [Elijah] came to a broom tree, sat down under it and prayed that he might die. 'I have had enough, Lord,' he said. 'Take my life; I am no better than my ancestors.'" *1 Kings 19:4*

Jonah, in his anger and weakness, said that he wanted to die. "He [Jonah] wanted to die, and said, 'It would be better for me to die than to live.'" *Jonah 4:8*

Suicides solve nothing

The main reason that Christians disapprove of suicide so much is that our lives are a gift from God and so it is not up to us to end our own lives.

If you were to ask a family in which a suicide has taken place they would tell you that the suicide solved nothing.

Paul

Some people have taken Paul's words in Philippians chapter 1 to mean that suicide is permissible for a Christian. But this is not the case. Paul knew that after this life he would be even closer to Jesus, which is "better" than living this life. But Paul did not commit suicide. One reason he states for carrying on living is for the sake of other Christians. See Philippians 1:21-26.

Swearing and the Christian

Bible principles about swearing
1. Blasphemy is out
No Christian should use language that takes the Lord's name in vain. This is clearly taught in the Ten Commandments. "You shall not misuse the name of the Lord your God, for the Lord will not hold anyone guiltless who misuses his name." *Exodus 20:7*

2. Swearing is out as well
In the context of taking oaths Jesus said, "Do not swear at all."

"Do not swear at all: either by heaven, for it is God's throne; or by the earth, for it is his footstool; for by Jerusalem, for it is the city of the Great King. And do not swear by your head, for you cannot make even one hair white or black. Simply let your 'Yes' be 'Yes,' and your 'No,' 'No;' anything beyond this comes from the evil one." *Matthew 5:34-37*

Everyday life
Question:
Will I be condemned if I let slip the odd "damn"?
Answer:
This question rather misses the point. For we are to take swearing seriously. Jesus said that it comes from the evil one.

Question:
I've sworn and blasphemed all my life, and have been with people who are just the same. What am I to do? How can I give up this way of life?

Answer:
You will find it much more difficult not to swear than people who have not been brought up in an environment where swearing and blasphemy is the order of the day. However, you should still make it your aim not to swear, even if you often fail. If your heart really wants to be close to God that is the most important thing. Ask Jesus to help you about swearing and blasphemy.

Question:
Did anyone other than Jesus say it is wrong to swear?
Answer:
Yes. James wrote, "Above all, my brothers, do not swear – not by heaven or by earth or by anything else. Let your 'Yes' be yes, and your 'No,' no, or you will be condemned." *James 5:12*

4 *SOCIAL RELATIONSHIPS*

CONTENTS	
	page
INTRODUCTION	121
SOCIAL ACTION AND THE BIBLE	122
CHRISTIANS AND TOTAL WELFARE	123
COMMUNITY INVOLVEMENT	124-125
POLITICAL INVOLVEMENT	126-131
WEALTH: BECOME POOR	132-133
WEALTH: STAY RICH	134-135
WEALTH: THE CHRISTIAN ATTITUDE	136-137
CAPITAL PUNISHMENT: SHOULD IT BE OUTLAWED?	138-143
WORK	144-149
EUTHANASIA	150-163

Introduction

The Bible lays down solid and essential foundations about moral issues, giving principles that act as overriding considerations when making moral choices. In the light of biblical teaching we can ask the following questions about any intended action:

- How may it affect others?
- How will it affect my relationship with God?
- How will it affect me?

In many ways Christians have not, and still do not have, a particularly good track record when it comes to giving a biblical moral lead. For some Christians expend considerable energy attacking each other's teaching on moral issues. One of our problems revolves around Christians disagreeing on what is essential and what is non-essential, and what is so important that it must not be tolerated.

Jesus and moral teaching

According to the Gospels, many moral issues were brought to Jesus for his judgment: some by genuine enquirers, some as test cases by opponents seeking reason to condemn him. And Jesus very often laid down moral principles based on the teaching of the Old Testament. He insisted that his followers should ignore the ungodly traditional teaching of men and should abide by the eternally true teaching of God. Jesus reprimanded the Pharisees and teachers of the law for letting go of the commands of God and for holding on to the traditions of men (see Mark 7:8).

In his moral teaching, Jesus always went to the heart of the matter. In the Sermon on the Mount he emphasized the spiritual nature of God's laws. You may not be murderers, Jesus said, in effect, but anger will also be judged by God (see Matthew 5:21-23).

Social action and the Bible

Yes or no?

Some Christians have questioned whether it is right for them to be involved in social action. They are convinced about the necessity and priority in preaching the good news about Jesus to the whole world, but hesitate about being involved in social action. This has sprung from the fear that the gospel and evangelism might be watered down or even replaced by the social gospel.

A wake-up call

"All evangelicals [are] to stand openly and firmly for racial equality, human freedom, and all forms of social justice throughout the world."
Wheaton Declaration, 1966

"Evangelism and compassionate service belong together in the mission of God." *National Evangelical Anglican Congress, 1967*

"For the gospel is the root, of which both evangelism and social responsibility are the fruits."
Evangelism and Social Responsibility: An Evangelical Commitment, 1982

"So many of the soundest and most orthodox Christians go through this world in the spirit of the priest and the Levite in our Lord's parable."
J.I. Packer

What does the Bible say?

1. RELIGION INCLUDES LOOKING AFTER THE DISADVANTAGED
"Religion that God our Father accepts as pure and faultless is this: to look after the orphans and widows in their distress."
James 1:27

2. THE GOD OF THE BIBLE IS A GOD OF COMPASSION
"He upholds the cause of the oppressed
    and gives food to the hungry.
The Lord sets prisoners free,
    the Lord gives sight to the blind,
The Lord lifts up those who are bowed down,
    the Lord loves the righteous.
The Lord watches over the alien
    and sustains the fatherless and the widow…"
Psalm 146:7-9

3. FAITH AND LOVE GO HAND IN HAND
"In the same way, faith by itself, if it is not accompanied by action, is dead. But someone will say, 'You have faith; I have deeds.' Show me your faith without deeds, and I will show you my faith by what I do."
James 2:17, 18

Christians and total welfare

"A body-soul-in-community"

"A human being might be defined from a biblical perspective as 'a body-soul-in-community.' For that is how God has made us. So if we truly love our neighbors, and because of their worth desire to serve them, we shall be concerned for their total welfare, the well-being of their soul, body and community." *John Stott*

I WAS HUNGRY

After a homeless person had been told by a Christian pastor that he would pray for her she wrote:

"I was hungry,
   and you formed a humanities group
   to discuss my hunger.
I was imprisoned,
   and you crept off quietly to your
   chapel and prayed for my release.
I was naked,
   and in your mind you debated the
   morality of my appearance.
I was sick,
   and you knelt and thanked God for
   your health.
I was homeless,
   and you preached to me of the
   spiritual shelter of the love of God.
I was lonely,
   and you left me alone to pray
   for me.
You seem so holy, so close to God
   But I am still very hungry – and
   lonely – and cold."

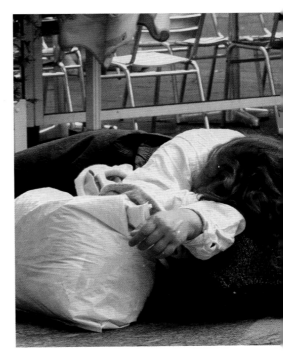

A glance at Christians and social action in history

- The early Christians took care of widows.
- Christians have often been in the forefront of founding hospitals, schools and refuges for the outcast.
- Christians have campaigned to reform the inhuman conditions of prisons, mines and mills.
- Christians led the way in caring for and using reconstructive surgery on leprosy sufferers.
- Christians were first in the field in the modern hospice movement.

Community involvement

The sheep and the goats

In Jesus' famous words about the sheep and the goats, a question is asked at its end: "Lord, when did we see you hungry or thirsty or a stranger or needing clothes or sick or in prison, and did not help you?"

The reply to this question is: "I tell you the truth, whatever you did not do for one of the least of these, you did not do for me." And then Jesus added these sober words in conclusion: "Then they will go away to eternal punishment, but the righteous to eternal life."

Matthew 25:44-46

Where were you Christians?

During some periods of history Christians have been all too conspicuous by their absence from the front-line of social work, while at other times they have been in the forefront of such ministry.

Life Magazine

On 13 March 1964 *Life* Magazine reported a frightening example of irresponsible detachment in New York.

A decent pretty young woman of 28 called Kitty Genovese was returning home from her job as manager for a bar.

It was 3.20 a.m. She had parked her car and was walking the remaining few yards to her apartment, when she was attacked by a man and stabbed. She screamed for help. Several lights went on in the apartment block, and somebody shouted from an upper window, "Let the girl alone."

The assailant looked up, shrugged his shoulders and walked off. But as the lights went out again and nobody came to her rescue, he returned and stabbed her a second time. At her renewed screams more lights went on, windows were opened and heads looked out. So the man got into his car and drove away. But again, as nobody came to help her, he returned to stab her for the third time and kill her. Not until 3.50 a.m. did the police receive their first phone call. By then Kitty was dead.

When the police questioned local residents, they found that at least 38 respectable middle-class, law-abiding citizens had heard the woman's screams, and had watched her being stabbed, but not one had done anything about it. She had even recognized one witness and called him by name, but he did not reply.

Why, the police asked, had these people not come to her aid? Some confessed that they did not know. A housewife said she "thought it was a lover's quarrel."

A man explained without emotion, "I was tired. I went back to bed."

"But the word we kept hearing from the witnesses," said Police Lieutenant Bernard Jacobs, "was 'involved'. People told us they just didn't want to get involved."

Good neighbors

Jesus ended one of his most famous parables with the question: "Which of these three do you think was a neighbor to the man who fell into the hands of robbers?" *Luke 10:36.* When the expert in the law replied, "The one who had mercy on him," Jesus said, "Go and do likewise."

Trevor Farrel

In 1983, when he was 11 years old, Trevor Farrel saw a television program about the plight of homeless people in Philadelphia, which was about 18 miles from his home. Trevor persuaded his parents to drive him there with a blanket and a pillow to give to a homeless person. Each night after that they drove into the city, until they had nothing to give away.

Then Trevor advertized the needs of the homeless in Philadelphia and asked for gifts and old blankets, pillows and warm clothes. His story was taken up by a television station and a newspaper. So many gifts came in that a warehouse had to be found to hold everything. A church gave a shelter with 33 rooms, which they called "Trevor's Place." Within two years 250 people were joining Trevor and his parents each night to serve hot meals to the homeless.

Political involvement

TOTAL ABOLITION OUGHT TO TAKE PLACE

Speech in House of Commons, London, 1789

I mean not to accuse anyone but to take the shame upon myself, in common indeed with the whole Parliament of Great Britain, for having suffered this horrid trade to be carried on under their authority. We are all guilty - we ought all to plead guilty, and not to exculpate ourselves by throwing the blame on others...

It is not regulation, it is not mere palliatives, that can cure this enormous evil: total Abolition is the only possible cure for it...I trust I have shown that upon every ground the total Abolition ought to take place...[Wilberforce then explained his motivation in being an abolitionist.] There is a principle, and I am not ashamed to say. There is a principle above everything that is political. And when I reflect on the command that says, 'Thou shalt do no murder,' believing the authority to be divine, how can I dare set up any reasonings of my own against it? And, Sir, when we think of eternity, and of the future consequences of all human conduct, where is there in this life which should make any man contradict the principles of his own conscience, the principles of justice, the laws of religion, and of God?

Sir, the nature and all the circumstances of the Trade are now laid open to us. We can no longer plead ignorance, we cannot evade it, it is now an object placed before us, we cannot pass it. We may spurn it, we may kick it out of our way, but we cannot turn aside so as to avoid seeing it. For it is brought now so directly before our eyes that this House must decide, and must justify to all the world, and to their own consciences, the rectitudes of their grounds and of the principles of their decision...Let not Parliament be the only body that is insensible to natural justice. Let us make reparation to Africa, so far as we can, by establishing a trade upon true commercial principles, and we shall soon find the rectitude of our conduct rewarded by the benefits of a regular and a growing commerce.
William Wilberforce

Can Christianity and politics mix?

Some Christians have maintained that Christians should steer clear of politics. It has been argued that Jesus went about preaching and doing good and did not found a political party.

However, Jesus did say to his followers that they were meant to be the salt and light of their society. These verses in Matthew 5:13-16 come in the Sermon on the Mount, directly after the beatitudes.

William Wilberforce

Some Christians believe that God called them to serve him and humanity through a career in politics. William Wilberforce, 1759-1833, was one such Christian. Sir Reginald Coupland wrote of him, that in order to break the apathy of Parliament, he "must possess the virtues of a fanatic without his vices. He must be palpably single-minded and unself-seeking. He must be strong enough to face opposition and ridicule, staunch enough to endure obstruction and delay."

Irremediable wickedness

In 1787 Wilberforce decided to present his motion about the slave trade to the House of Commons. His proposed bill met with strong opposition at every point. In 1789 Wilberforce said in the House, "So enormous, so dreadful, so irremediable did its wickedness appear that my own mind was completely made up for Abolition. Let the consequences be what they would, I from this time determined that I would never rest until I had effected Abolition."

Failure after failure

Wilberforce debated in the Commons the Abolition Bills, which were about the slave trade itself, and Foreign Slave Bills, which were about the involvement of British ships in it, in 1789, 1791, 1792, 1794, 1796, 1798 and 1799. Each time the bills met with such opposition from vested interest that they failed.

After 18 years

It was not until 1806 that the Foreign Slave Bill was passed and the Slave Trade Bill in 1807. Wilberforce had persevered in the teeth of bitter opposition for 18 years.

Wilberforce then set about abolishing the slave trade itself and emancipating the slaves. The Anti-Slavery Society was formed in 1823. Twice in 1823 and twice in 1824 Wilberforce tried, without success, to persuade the House of Commons to pass a law to abolish slavery. In 1825 ill-health forced Wilberforce to retire as a member of parliament.

But that year he wrote to the Anti-Slavery Society, "Our motto must continue to be *perseverence*. And ultimately I trust the Almighty will crown our efforts with success."

45 years of perseverence

In July 1833 the Abolition of Slavery Bill was passed, but with the provision that £20,000,000 would be given in compensation to slave-owners. Wilberforce wrote, "Thank God that I have lived to witness a day in which England is willing to give £20,000,000 for the abolition of slavery." Wilberforce died three days later. He had spent 45 years working on behalf of African slaves.

Born-again Christians were in the forefront off every major social reform in America during the 1830s. They spear-headed the abolitionist movement, the temperance movement, the peace movement, and the early feminist movement.

Charles G. Finney

John Wesley and William Wilberforce

The last letter that John Wesley wrote was to William Wilberforce, who had been converted under Wesley's ministry. The letter concerns Wesley's opposition to slavery and encouragement for Wilberforce to take action for change. Parliament finally outlawed England's participation in the slave trade in 1807.

Founder of the Salvation Army

Shortly before his death, William Booth made his last speech, from which this extract is taken.

> "While women weep, as they do now,
>   I'll fight;
> while men go to prison, in and out,
>   as they do now, I'll fight;
> while there is a drunkard left,
> while there is a poor lost girl upon the
>   streets,
> where there remains one dark soul
>   without the love of God – I'll fight!
> I'll fight to the very end."
> *William Booth*

Helping Christian politicians

We need to help people who hold biblical values, and especially to our lawmakers. In this way Isaiah's rebuke should not be true of our own society: "Woes to those who make unjust laws, to those who issue oppressive decrees, to deprive the poor of their rights and withhold from the oppressed of my people." *Isaiah 10:1*

BALHAM, FEBRUARY 24 1791

Dear Sir:

Unless the divine power has raised you up to be as *Athanasius contra mundum*, (Athanasius against the world), I see not how you can go through your glorious enterprise in opposing that execrable villainy which is the scandal of religion, of England, and of human nature. Unless God has raised you up for this very thing, you will be worn out by the opposition of men and devils. But if God be for you, who can be against you? Are all of them together stronger than God? O be not weary of well doing! Go on, in the name of God and in the power of his might, till even American slavery (the vilest that ever saw the sun) shall vanish away before it.

Reading this morning a tract wrote by a poor African, I was particularly struck by that circumstance that a man who has a black skin, being wronged or outraged by a white man, can have no redress; it being a "law" in our colonies that the oath of a black against a white goes for nothing. What villainy is this?

That he who has guided you from youth up may continue to strengthen you in this and all things, is the prayer of, dear sir,

Your affectionate servant,

John Wesley

Wealth: become poor

Option number one: become poor
See also Stewardship: pages 116-117.

Some people are called to give up everything
Should all Christians be like Francis of Assisi? He believed that God called him to live a life of poverty. So he spent his life in serving the poor and assisting the sick.

After all, Jesus himself said: "Any of you who does not give up everything he has cannot be my disciple" Luke 14:33. This is exactly what Jesus' first disciples did. James and John and Andrew and Peter left their fishing business and followed Jesus.

To the rich young man who came to Jesus with a question about how to inherit eternal life, Jesus said: "Go, sell everything you have and give to the poor, and you will have treasure in heaven. Then come, follow me" Mark 10:21.

THE DANGER OF BEING POSSESSED BY RICHES
"There is nothing wrong with people possessing riches. The wrong comes when riches possess people."
Billy Graham

But not everyone was told to become poor
Jesus never made it a universal rule that all his followers should give away all their wealth and money and property and then follow him.

Joseph of Aramathea
The little we know about the man who buried Jesus' body with Nicodemus is that he was "a rich man," Matthew 27:57, and "a disciple of Jesus," John 19:38.

Zacchaeus
Zacchaeus was a very rich chief tax-collector. After his conversion he gave away half of his wealth and paid back to people he had cheated four times what he had taken. This still left him with a considerable amount of money. Jesus said of Zacchaeus, "'Today salvation has come to this house'" Luke 19:9.

What about the example of the early church?
If we wanted to make out a case that all Christians should hand over all their real estate to the local church fellowship their appears much to support this idea in the record of how the first Christians behaved, as we read it in Acts.

- All the believers…had everything in common, see Acts 2:44
- Selling their possessions and goods, see Acts 2:45
- they gave to anyone as he had need, see Acts 2:45
- No one claimed that any of his possessions was his own, see Acts 4:32
- but they shared everything they had, see Acts 4:32. This resulted in there being

- no needy persons among them, see Acts 4:34.
- They gave to anyone as he had need.

Questions to ask

Was this giving away of possessions universal?

Was this giving away of possessions compulsory?

Ananias and Sapphira

In the incident of Ananias and Sapphira, Acts 5:1-11, Peter challenged them: "Didn't it [the land they sold] belong to you before it was sold? And after it was sold, wasn't the money at your disposal?" Acts 5:4. There is no hint here that Christians did anything wrong by owning land. Nor is there any hint that they were under compulsion to give away any of the money if they did sell the land.

In addition to this, some of the early Christians had houses, where they met for Christian fellowship, or just used as homes to live in, see Acts 2:2; 20:40.

Conclusion

Some Christians today may be called by God to sell up and give everything to the poor.

All Christians are called to look after the poor and after fellow-Christians.

There is no commandment that all Christians must sell all their possessions and give the proceeds to God's work.

Wealth: stay rich

Option number two: stay rich

If the Bible does not teach that all Christians must become poor the idea that Christians should stay rich seems to have special appeal today.

God's blessing and being rich

Some Christians link God's blessing with acquiring and keeping vast piles of money. They see that wealth is a sign of God's blessing, and they encourage other Christians to think and act in this way.

Does not Deuteronomy 28:8 say, "The Lord will send a blessing on your barns and on everything you put your hand to"?

Physical and spiritual blessings

When Israel, God's people, was a nation God did indeed promise to bless them materially in response to them obeying him. Today Christians should perhaps rather emphasize the spiritual riches we have in Jesus, who has blessed us "with every spiritual blessing" Ephesians 1:3.

Neglect

In the Old Testament, as much as in the New Testament, we are commanded to look after the poor. The rich man, Dives, in Jesus' parable, see Luke 16:19-31, ended up in hell, not because he was rich, but because he neglected to help the starving man, Lazarus.

Staying rich is not a Christian option

It can hardly be right, as we live in a world where millions of people lack the most basic necessities of life, for wealthy Christians to ignore the poor and destitute, instead of radically altering their life of luxury.

Paul's teaching about the rich

"Command those who are rich in this present world not to be arrogant nor to put their hope in wealth, which is so uncertain, but to put their hope in God, who richly provides us with everything for our enjoyment. Command them to do good, to be rich in good deeds, and to be generous and willing to share. In this way they will lay up treasure for themselves as a firm foundation for the coming age, so that they may take hold of the life that is truly life."
1 Timothy 6:17-19

Two dangers of staying rich
1. The danger of pride
"Command those who are rich in this present world not to be arrogant." Wealth often makes people feel arrogant and contemptuous of others. See James 2:1-7.

2. The danger of materialism
"Command those who are rich...nor to put their hope in wealth, which is so uncertain, but to put their hope in God."

Being rich does not automatically mean that we are materialistic. But we become materialistic when we are obsessed by our wealth. If we place our trust in our bank balance, stocks and shares, income, or real estate, instead of in Jesus, then we have already become materialistic.

Question:
But is not God the one "who richly provides us with everything for our enjoyment"?
Answer:
This is true and for this reason the cure for materialism is not asceticism. For being austere for its own sake does not acknowledge that all good gifts come from the hand of our Creator. The danger the wealthy face is that our relationship to God and our relationship with our fellow human beings is likely to be spoiled. This happens when we forget God and despise the poor. "If you have wealth, do not glory in it."
Thomas à Kempis

Wealth: the Christian attitude

Be generous

"Command those who are rich in this present world…to be rich in good deeds" 1 Timothy 6:17-18. Anyone who is generous with their money and possessions is imitating God who is himself so generous that he "richly provides us with everything for our enjoyment."

We can test our own generosity against the following question, which the apostle John posed: "If anyone has material possessions, and sees his brother in need, but has no pity on him, how can the love of God be in him?" *1 John 3:17*

Be content

"But godliness with contentment is great gain. For we brought nothing into the world, and we can take nothing out of it. But if we have food and clothing, we will be content with that. People who want to get rich fall into temptation and a trap and into many foolish and harmful desires that plunge men into ruin and destruction. For the love of money is a root of all kinds of evil. Some people, eager for money, have wandered from the faith and pierced themselves with many griefs." *1 Timothy 6:6-10*

"The people who want to get rich" are often covetous people. In contrast to the danger of covetousness, Paul urges rich people to be content.

"Gold is like sea water – the more one drinks of it, the thirstier one becomes." *Schopenhauer*

Christian contentment springs from our knowledge of God, not from having possessions. That is why "godliness with contentment is great gain."

Go for simplicity

For a Christian having a lifestyle governed by simplicity means that "if we have food and clothing, we will be content with that" 1 Timothy 6:8.

Proverbs captures the idea of a simple lifestyle in Proverbs 30:8, "give me

neither poverty nor riches, but give me only my daily bread."

"Those of us who live in affluent circumstances accept our duty to develop a simple lifestyle, in order to contribute more generously to both relief and evangelism...[We resolve] to renounce waste and oppose extravagance in: personal living, clothing and housing, travel and church buildings."
The Lausanne Covenant – An Exposition and Commentary

Choices

If we decide to go in for a more simple lifestyle that should gives us a different perspective on the numerous everyday choices we make.

Personal questions that need to be answered

- Should we increase our giving as our income rises?
- Should we move home just because we can afford to move into a bigger house?
- Should my will include any donations to Christian causes?
- Should our lifestyle be changed in any way in the light of global poverty?
- Should our Christian fellowship spend hundreds of thousands of dollars in repairs/extensions to our church buildings?
- Should we be slaves to fashion all the time? If we do decide against always desiring to acquire the latest "in" thing how could our purchases of clothes and other possessions change over the next 12 months?
- How should our investments reflect our beliefs in ethical/Christian principles?
- Should we own any shares in companies that produce cigarettes or exploit the poor, or in companies that deplete poor countries of their irreplaceable resources, or in fast-food organizations which use animals which have been reared in cruel conditions?

Capital punishment: should it be outlawed?

Key verse

Capital punishment is no new idea. It is commanded in the early chapters of Genesis. "Whoever sheds the blood of man, by man shall his blood be shed; for in the image of God has God made man." *Genesis 9:6*

Questions

Is there a biblical basis for capital punishment today, or was the death penalty only to be practiced in Old Testament times?

Since Romans 10:4 says that "Christ is the end of the Law," is there any possible ground on which to justify capital punishment in the twenty-first century?

Why can't all countries be like Canada? During the last decade of the twentieth century, 547 prisoners were executed in the United States – one third of them in Texas. Another 3,500 wait on death rows. None have been executed in Canada where the death penalty was abolished decades ago.

Quotations *against* capital punishment

FORMER EXECUTION OFFICER

"As I read the New Testament, I don't see anywhere in there that killing bad people is a very high calling for Christians. I see an awful lot about redemption and forgiveness."
James W. L. Park, former execution officer, San Quentin, California

CANADA

"In Canada, the death penalty has been rejected as an acceptable element of criminal justice. Capital punishment engages the underlying values of the prohibition against cruel and unusual punishment. It is final and irreversible. Its imposition has been described as arbitrary and its deterrent value has been doubted."
Supreme Court of Canada, "United States v. Burns," 15 Feb 2001

Arguments *against* capital punishment

1. To take the life of another person can never be right.
2. No matter how terrible a crime has been committed a life for a life can never justified.
3. Capital punishment applied in ancient Israel when the nation was a theocracy, directly under God's rule. But God no longer is in direct rule of any nation now. Therefore, there is no longer any basis for the death penalty.
4. God would never put the power over life and death into the hands of imperfect man.
5. Capital punishment is not a complete deterrent against people committing murder.
6. Don't the "love your enemy" teachings of Jesus remove the "eye for eye, tooth for tooth, life for life" requirements of the Mosaic Law?

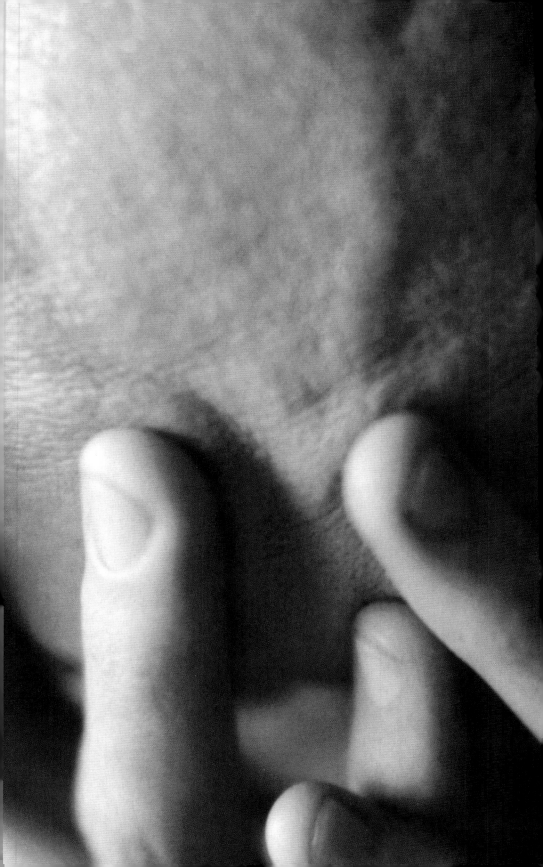

7. Isn't restorative justice more in line with the teaching of the New Testament?

Arguments *in favor* of capital punishment

It is admitted that wherever capital punishment has been used miscarriages of justice have occurred and innocent people have been sentenced to death and killed.

It is also agreed that the crime of murder has never been eradicated by capital punishment.

1. The threat of capital punishment, wherever it has been in force, has deterred some people from committing murder. For example, in Islamic countries, where "eye for eye, tooth for tooth, life for life" laws are literally carried out the crime rate is lower than the crime rate of western nations where there is no death sentence to enforce.
2. The biblical basis for capital punishment remains strong and does not change.

The death penalty and the laws under Moses

In the days of Moses capital punishment was a civil law. Israel, which was then under God's direct rule, as a theocracy, had the responsibility to maintain civil law and order. Part of this law included capital punishment. Capital punishment applied to many more offences than it does today.

21 offenses

21 different offenses called for the death penalty in the Old Testament.

Under the Law, the sins of:

- adultery
- incest
- homosexuality
- bestiality
- witchcraft
- idolatry

were punishable by death. See Leviticus 20:1-27.

Even a profligate, drunken, and rebellious teenager who would not submit to the authority of his parents was to be stoned to death! See Deuteronomy 21:18-21.

However, the civil requirements of the Mosaic covenant are no longer in force, so where does that leave us concerning a biblical basis for capital punishment?

But, the biblical basis for capital punishment is not the covenant made to Moses!

Go back to Genesis

To find the most important teaching about the death penalty in the Bible we need to go back to the book of Genesis.

The original biblical basis for capital punishment is found in the covenant that was given to Noah. The laws in this covenant apply to every generation who follow Noah. This is stated in Genesis 9:12. There this covenant God made with Noah was also for "all generations to come."

The sign of God's covenant with Noah was, and still is, the rainbow, Genesis 9:13. So long as there are rainbows in the sky, God's covenant with Noah is still in effect, Genesis 9:14-17. Capital punishment was commanded by God in Genesis 9:6.

The covenant with Noah and capital punishment

One of the stipulations of God's covenant with Noah was capital punishment.

But Genesis 9:6 states that the death penalty only applied to the crime of murder. It did not apply to all the other sins listed in God's covenant with Moses.

Why was the death penalty given?

Genesis 9:6 refers to a murderer, one who knowingly and violently sheds another man's blood, resulting in death. God gives man the authority, even the right and the duty, to execute the murderer: "by man shall his blood be shed."

The reason given for this is based upon the value and sacredness of human life: "for in the image of God has God made man."

This command concerning the death penalty was based on the dignity of man, that humans are greatly valued in God's sight. Yes, contradictory as it seems at first sight, capital punishment was instituted because God places a very high value on human life!

God views human life to be so valuable that he commanded that those who take human life must suffer the ultimate punishment – the death penalty.

What about "Thou shalt not kill"?

Is not capital punishment a violation of the sixth commandment which says, "Thou shalt not kill" Exodus 20:13?

A more meaningful and accurate translation of Exodus 20:13 would be, "Thou shalt not murder." The *NIV*, for example, says, "You shall not murder."

The *King James Version* says in Matthew 19:18, "Thou shalt do no murder."

All murder is killing but not all killing is murder

There are a number of examples of killing that should not be considered as murder:

- Killing the enemy in war. Bible examples of this are David killing Goliath, and Joshua and the Israelites when they conquered the land.
- Killing an intruder who was about to kill your family.
- A policeman who kills in the line of duty in order to protect innocent life
- An executioner carrying out capital punishment.

The teaching of the New Testament

Capital punishment, based on God's covenant with Noah, was never changed by Jesus. The relevant teaching of the New Testament about the death penalty can be found in Romans 13:1-5; 1 Peter 2:13-14.

The sword

Romans 13:1 states, "Everyone must submit himself to the governing authorities, for there is no authority except that which God has established." Then in Romans 13:4 Paul says that these civil authorities do "not bear the *sword* for nothing."

It is implied here that the state has a God-given power, even though it may be open to abuse, of life and death over its subjects.

"Through the state there takes place a partial, anticipatory, provisional manifestation of God's wrath against sin" *C. E. B. Cranfield*

It is clear that even though Paul was referring to the godly government of Nero, governments may practice capital punishment.

How far should capital punishment go?

In Genesis the basis for the use of the death penalty only applied to the crime of murder. So any government today should not extend the death penalty to apply to any other crime.

Law and order

There are numerous law and order questions that affect us each day. From general biblical principles we need to work out our attitude to any of the following questions which are relevant to us:

- Should we consider becoming foster parents to children born in dreadful circumstances?
- Should we consider adopting a teenager who has been in and out of penal institutions?
- Should we consider becoming prison visitors?
- Should we consider supporting Christian organizations that minister in prisons?
- Should we actively seek to help ex-prisoners find a job?
- Should we lobby against reforms to our laws, which break Christian ideals?

Work

Attitudes to work

NOT TODAY

"I don't mind work
If I've nothing else to do;
I quite admit it's true
That now and then I shirk
Particularly boring kinds of work;
Don't you?
But, on the whole,
I think it's fair to say
Provided I can do it my own way
And that I need not start on it today–
I quite like work!"
Author unknown

"I like work; it fascinates me.
I can sit and look at it for hours."
Jerome K. Jerome

HARD WORK

"In the sweat of thy face shalt thou
eat bread."
Genesis 3:19, KJV

"Man goeth forth unto his work and
to his labor until the evening."
Psalm 104:23, KJV

"Whatsoever thy hand findeth to do,
do it with thy might."
Ecclesiastes 9:10, KJV

"If it is to be, it is up to me!"
Author unknown

"The only place where success comes
before work is in the dictionary."
Author unknown

"Plans are only good intentions
unless they immediately degenerate
into hard work."
Peter F. Drucker

IDLENESS

"She looketh well to the ways of her
household, and eateth not the bread
of idleness."
Proverbs 31:17, KJV

"We can't all, and some of us don't.
That's all there is to it."
Eeyore (A.A. Milne)

A FAIR DAY'S WORK FOR A FAIR DAY'S PAY
"The laborer is worthy of his hire."
Luke 7:1

ACCOMPLISHING WORK
"Nothing is particularly hard if you divide it into small jobs."
Henry Ford

WORKING FOR THE LORD
"Whatever you do, work at it with all your heart, as working for the Lord, not for men."
Colossians 3:23

"A servant with this clause
Makes drudgery divine;
Who sweeps a room as for Thy laws
Makes that and th' action fine."
George Herbert

"Do no activity which you cannot entitle God to, and truly say that he set you about it, and do nothing in the world for any other ultimate purpose than to please, glorify and enjoy Him. 'Whatever you do, do all to the glory of God'
1 Corinthians 10:31." Richard Baxter

"Work becomes worship when done for the Lord."
Author unknown

WORK IS...
"Genius is 1% inspiration and 99% perspiration."
Author unknown

EVERY LITTLE HELPS
"Nobody made a greater mistake than he who did nothing because he could only do a little."
Edmund Burke

"Let us not cease to do the utmost, and go forward in the way of the Lord; and let us not despair of the smallness of our accomplishments."
John Calvin

THE GOAL OF WORK
"Work to become, not to acquire."
Confucius

CO-OPERATING WITH GOD
"A servant with this clause
Makes drudgery divine;
Who sweeps a room as for Thy laws
Makes that and the action fine."
George Herbert

THE DIGNITY OF WORK
"The trivial round, the common task
Will furnish all we ought to ask;
Room to deny ourselves – a road
To bring us daily nearer God."
John Keble

Work and self-fulfillment

One aspect of self-fulfillment should be found in our work. God told Adam and Eve: "Be fruitful and increase in number; fill the earth and subdue it" Genesis 1:28. All human beings have a vocation for work. Ideally this work should be creative work as God has made us creative creatures.

"Work is not primarily a thing one does to live, but the thing one lives to do."
Dorothy Sayers

"Work is one of the characteristics that distinguish man from the rest of creatures...Work is a good thing for man because through it he achieves fulfillment as a human being, and indeed, in sense, becomes more a human being."
Pope John Paul II, Laborem Exercens

"Thank God that you have something to do which must be done, whether you like it or not. Being forced to work, and forced to do your best, will breed in you a hundred virtues which the idle never know."
Charles Kingsley

Serving God and humankind through work

E. F. Shumacher gives the following three purposes for work:

"First, to provide necessary and useful goods and services.

Second, to enable every one of us to use the thereby perfect our gifts like good stewards.

Third, to do so in service to, and in co-operation with others, so as to liberate ourselves from our inborn egocentricity."

The best vision one can have for work is to view it as being for God's glory. Martin Luther expressed this ideal as follows: "God even milks the cows through you."

The sixteenth-century French surgeon, Ambroise Paré, known as "the founder of modern surgery," had inscribed the following words on the wall of the École de Médicine in Paris: "I dressed the wound, but God healed him."

Work is meant to be for the glory of God: "So whether you eat or drink or whatever you do, do it all for the glory of God." *1 Corinthians 10:31*

"Let us work as if success depended upon ourselves alone; but with heartfelt conviction that we are doing nothing and God everything." *Ignatius Loyola*

Honesty at work

In theory Christians are agreed that
honesty is the best policy. However, our
high Christian moral standards
sometimes drop when it comes to work.

Pinching paperclips

Does it matter if I take home paper and
envelopes from the office? And what
about using the office phone for private
calls?

"Well," we might think, "this is hardly
a terrible action, but, I suppose, if you
were being very strict you might label
this as stealing." In many large retail
shops up to 5% of the takings are
unaccounted for every day. The money
disappears into the pockets of the shop
assistants, and the accountants just write
this off, calling it "shrinkage."

Some Christians give the appearance
of being like the worst of the Pharisees.
Some Pharisees were meticulous about
keeping the law down to the last detail,
even tithing the herbs they grew. Some
Christians seem to adopt a "holier-than-
thou" attitude, but all the time are
themselves devoid of basic Christian
characteristics. This is what Jesus said:
"Woe to you, teachers of the law and
Pharisees, you hypocrites! You give a
tenth of your spices – mint, dill and

cummin. But you have neglected the more important matters of the law – justice, mercy and faithfulness. You should have practiced the latter, without neglecting the former. You blind guides! You strain out a gnat but swallow a camel." *Matthew 23:23, 24*

Calling in sick

Does it matter if I call in sick when I want an extra, unofficial day off?

"Well," we might think, "everybody seems to do this, so why shouldn't Christians? But, I suppose, you could say that is was technically 'stealing' time from the employer."

Dropping my mates in it

If everyone else in my section is putting in for overtime that they did not do, should I do the same? On the grounds of honesty, we might conclude that we should not. But what if that will blow the whistle on all those I work with? Should a Christian be so "honest" that this leads other people into trouble?

Is it okay to be ambitious?

Should I be ambitious at work? Is it right to seek promotion?

There are dangers here. It is possible to seek a better job just to satisfy one's greed. It is possible to become a workaholic and just to live for work. Some people are so absorbed in their work that their family, their church fellowship, not to say their own souls, suffer.

"There can be intemperance in work just as in drink."
C. S. Lewis

"One of the symptoms of an approaching nervous breakdown is the belief that one's work is terribly important."
Bertrand Russell

On the other hand, one does not have to have the top job in order to serve God faithfully at work. Some people are content to carry out seemingly menial and routine work and remain happy in their work.

However, the parable of the talents, Matthew 25:14-30, teaches that we should put our talents to work. In this sense we would be keen for promotion. But the point of being promoted is not just a fatter pay-packet, but to be faithful in taking on more responsibility. Luke 12:48 guides us here: "From everyone who has been given much, much will be demanded; and from the one who has been entrusted with much, much more will be asked."

Cromwell, I charge thee, fling away ambition:
    By that sin fell the angels. How can man then,
    The image of his maker, hope to win by it?
William Shakespeare, Henry VIII

Euthanasia

"Deception is not as creative as truth. We do best in life if we look at it with clear eyes, and I think that applies to coming up to death as well."
Cicely Saunders, founder of the modern hospice movement

The need for a consistent ethic of life
"Nuclear war threatens life on a previously unimaginable scale; abortion takes life daily on a horrendous scale. Euthanasia is now openly discussed and advocated [and has been written into the statute books in some countries]. This highlights the case for a consistent ethic of life. It calls for positive legal action to prevent the killing of the unborn or the aged and positive societal action to provide shelter for the homeless and education for the illiterate."
Joseph Bernardin

Only God
"Only God can decide life and death." *Mother Teresa*

In time...
"In time, they will start killing grown-up people, disabled people and so on." *Mother Teresa*

Scriptures to meditate on

"You shall not murder."
Exodus 20:13

"The Lord said to him [Moses], 'Who gave man his mouth? Who makes him deaf or mute? Who gives him sight or makes him blind? Is it not I, the Lord?'"
Exodus 4:11

"'Shall we not accept good from God, and not trouble?' In all this Job did not sin in what he said."
Job 2:10

"See now that I myself am He! There is no god besides me. I put to death and I bring to life, I have wounded, and I will heal, and no one can deliver out of my hand."
Deuteronomy 32:39

"There is a time for everything, and a season for every activity under heaven: a time to be born and a time to die."
Ecclesiastes 3:1, 2

What is euthanasia?
Euthanasia may be defined as: "The act or practice of ending the life of an individual suffering from a terminal illness or an incurable condition, as by lethal injection or the suspension of extraordinary medical treatment."

The word "euthanasia" literally means

"good death" or "easy death." Euthanasia is the act of killing, for reasons of mercy, people who are terminally ill or handicapped or very severely injured. Euthanasia often goes under the name of "mercy killing."

Mercy killing or murder?

Two questions:

- Is killing for reasons of mercy somehow less than killing?
- Isn't mercy killing just a euphemism for murder?

"Thou shalt not kill"

Everyone knows the sixth commandment: "Thou shalt not kill" Exodus 20:13; Deuteronomy 5:17, *KJV*. There are ten Hebrew words translated "kill" in the *King James Version* of the Bible. The one used in the sixth commandment is "*ratsach*" in Hebrew, and its Greek equivalent is "*phoneuo*." It is rightly translated as "murder." This is seen in Exodus 21:12-14; Leviticus 24:17-21; Numbers 35:16-31 and Deuteronomy 19:4-13.

A good way to define what the sixth commandment is prohibiting is: "intentional killing of an innocent human being." So the Old Testament teaching is that the intentional killing of any innocent human being is wrong. We note that there is:

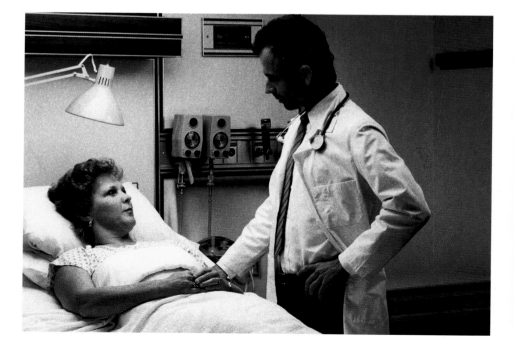

- no provision for diminished responsibility on the basis of age or illness
- no provision for compassionate killing even at the person's request
- no recognition of a "right to die."

Who does human life belong to?

- Human life belongs to God, Psalm 24:1: "The earth is the Lords, and everything in it."
- Life is not the personal possession of any human being.
- Only God has the authority to take human life.
- Man can only take a life under God's delegated authority.

The rise of euthanasia

In 1935 the Euthanasia Society of England was formed to promote the notion of a painless death for patients with incurable diseases. A few years later the Euthanasia Society of America was formed with similar aims.

More recently, the acceptance of euthanasia has gained ground thanks to the work of Derek Humphry and Dr Jack Kevorkian.

Derek Humphry

Derek Humphry has used his prominence as head of the Hemlock Society to promote euthanasia. His book *Final Exit: The Practicalities of Self-Deliverance and Assisted Suicide for the Dying* became a bestseller and further influenced public opinion.

Pain control

"No decent human being would allow an animal to suffer without putting it out of its misery," argues renowned author Isaac Asimov in a critic's blurb for the bestselling suicide manual *Final Exit*. It continues, "It is only to human beings that human beings are so cruel as to allow them to live on in pain, in hopelessness, in living death, without moving a muscle to help them."

Describing his client's most recent case of assisted suicide, Michael Schwartz, the lawyer for Dr Jack Kevorkian, said the doctor was simply alleviating suffering in the only way left. Michael Schwartz stated, "This is a case of medicine. It is a situation where the object was to alleviate the pain and suffering for patients who wish to have that pain and suffering put to an end."

Out of date

This may have provided an argument in favor of assisted suicide ten or fifteen years ago. But medical advances in pain control now allow doctors to so completely soothe intense suffering that this argument for accepting euthanasia has become virtually useless.

According to Professor Robert Spitzer, a philosopher and authority on medical ethics: "Such significant advances have been made in the last two or three years by pain control experts that now it can be said with assurance that you will almost certainly not die an agonizing death. It can be said with assurance that total pain control may be had in the vast majority of the diseases leading to death."

Dr Cecily Saunders, the founder of the modern hospice movement, argues that "Advances in pain control management have made the euthanasia option completely unnecessary."

JACK KEVORKIAN

Jack Kevorkian has been instrumental in helping people commit suicide. His book *Prescription Medicide: The Goodness of Planned Death* describes his patented suicide machine, which he calls "the Mercitron."

THE MERCITRON

When Dr Jack Kevorkian was constructing the suicide machine that would help Janet Adkins kill herself in 1990, he gave it a name which he thought described its function: "the Mercitron."

It seems a strange name for a machine that manufactures death; but Kevorkian isn't the only one to use the name "mercy" to describe his trade. The popular term for physicians helping terminally ill patients to commit suicide is "mercy-killing." And there seems to be widespread consensus that when doctors assist some patients with suicide, they are doing a compassionate work.

When Jack Kevorkian used his Mercitron in 1990 on Janet Adkins of Portland, Oregon, to help her to kill herself he became headline news.

Euthanasia and Janet Adkins

Dr Jack Kevorkian and Janet Adkins met for dinner and then drove to a Volkswagen van where the machine waited. Jack Kevorkian placed an intravenous tube into Janet Adkins' arm and dripped a saline solution until she pushed a button, which delivered first a drug causing unconsciousness, and then a lethal drug that killed her.

Since then Jack Kevorkian has helped dozens of other people do the same.

Medical advances

In the light of medical advances, which now enable us to preserve and prolong human life far longer than in the past, the following questions are now asked:

- Why shouldn't an old person be allowed to die with dignity?
- Why shouldn't an old person even be persuaded to die with dignity?
- Why drag out the earthly existence of an elderly person who has already enjoyed a full and happy life?
- Isn't euthanasia rightly called "mercy killing" when it comes to a chronically ill person or to a severely injured person?
- After all, allowing a person to die by turning off a life-support machine will avoid so much needless pain, won't it?
- Why prolong the life of a baby who is born with major physical handicaps or severe mental retardation?

The Bible and euthanasia

For centuries Western culture in general and Christians in particular have believed in the sanctity of human life. But now the phrase "quality of life" seems to be replacing the principle of "sanctity of life."

The disabled, retarded and infirm used to be given a special place in God's world. Today some people's fitness for life is judged by physicians on the basis of a perceived quality of life or lack of such quality. Increasingly, life is not seen as sacred and worthy of being saved.

Scriptural principles

The word "euthanasia" is not listed in a biblical concordance. That does not mean to say that the Bible has nothing to say on the subject. There are scriptural principles laid down in God's Word for our instruction on this very difficult matter.

1. Killing the innocent

Obviously the Bible teaches that it is wrong to deliberately terminate the life of an innocent human being. This breaks the sixth commandment, Exodus 20:13.

2. The handicapped

But what if a human life is "less than normal"? In Exodus 4:11 God says to Moses that the presence of some kind of physical handicap does not in any way lower the value of human life. From this we deduce that it is not right to kill handicapped people of any age.

3. Extreme suffering

What about the person going through extreme suffering and experiencing intense pain? There are some guidelines to be gleaned from the book of Job about this.

Job's terrible condition is stated in Job 2:7, 8; 7:5; 13:28; 30:16-18, 30. Job's wife suggested that it would be better to curse God and die than to go on living in such a miserable and painful condition.

Job himself wanted to die; he even longed for death, Job 3:20-22. But Job chose to endure. His response was, "Shall we not accept good from God, and not trouble?" Job believed that his suffering was allowed by God.

It seems fair to conclude that to mercifully terminate a life because of suffering or pain is not justified. To wrongly take a human life is murder.

God's right

God has the right to terminate life. In Deuteronomy 32:39 the Lord says, "I put to death I and bring to life." See also Samuel 2:6 and Psalm 90:3. The giving and taking of human life are prerogatives which belong to God alone.

Ecclesiastes 3:1, 2 states that there is a time to die. God not only has the right to take a life but he has a time appointed for taking that life. Ecclesiastes 3:1-8 teaches that all the events of life are divinely appointed.

Christians rightly regard euthanasia or mercy killing as being wrong according

to biblical teaching. It has been described as nothing less that a euphemism for killing or murder.

What's wrong with the "right to die" lobby?

Christians should reject attempts by the modern euthanasia movement to promote a so-called "right to die."

For giving a person a right to die is tantamount to promoting suicide. Suicide is condemned in the Bible. Man is forbidden to murder and that includes murder of oneself. In addition to that, Christians are supposed to love others as they love themselves, Matthew 22:39; Ephesians 5:29. Implicit in this command is an assumption of self-love as well as love for others. Suicide hardly displays self-love.

Joni Eareckson Tada

The so-called "right to die" idea denies God the opportunity to work sovereignly within a shattered life.

When Joni Eareckson Tada realized that she would be spending the rest of her life as a quadriplegic, she asked in despair, "Why can't they just let me die?"

When her friend Diana, trying to provide comfort, said to her, "The past is dead, Joni; you're alive," Joni responded, "Am I? This isn't living."

But through God's grace Joni's despair gave way to her firm conviction that even her accident was within God's plan for her life. Now she shares with the world her firm conviction that "suffering

gets us ready for heaven."

God's purposes and our finite human understanding

The Bible teaches that God's purposes are beyond our understanding. Job's reply to the Lord shows his acknowledgment of God's purposes.

"I know that you can do all things; no plan of yours can be thwarted. You asked, 'Who is this that obscures my counsel without knowledge?' Surely I spoke of things I did not understand, things too wonderful for me to know." Job 42:2, 3

Isaiah 55:8, 9 reminds us of the difference between God's thinking and our understanding:

"For my thoughts are not your thoughts, neither are your ways my ways, declares the Lord. As the heavens are higher than the earth, so are my ways higher than your ways and my thoughts than your thoughts."

The Bible's view of death

Another foundational principle is a biblical view of death. Death is both unnatural and inevitable.

It is an unnatural intrusion into our lives as a result of the fall of humankind, Genesis 2:17. Death is the last enemy to be destroyed, 1 Corinthians 15:26, 56.

This is why Christians should reject humanistic ideas that assume death as nothing more than a natural transition.

However, the Bible also teaches that death is inevitable. There is "a time to be born and a time to die" Ecclesiastes 3:2. Death is a part of life and the doorway to another, better life.

When does death occur?

Is death a biological event or a spiritual event?

Modern medicine defines death primarily as a biological event. Scripture defines death as a spiritual event that has biological consequences.

Death, according to the Bible, occurs when the spirit leaves the body. "The dust returns to the ground it came from, and the spirit returns to God who gave it," Ecclesiastes 12:7. "As the body without the spirit is dead, so faith without deeds is dead," James 2:26.

A comatose patient may not be conscious, but from both a medical and biblical perspective he is very much alive, and treatment should be continued unless crucial vital signs and brain activity have ceased.

On the other hand, Christians must also reject the notion that everything must be done to save life at all costs.

Believers, knowing that to be at home in the body is to be away from the Lord, 2 Corinthians 5:6, long for the time when they will be absent from the body and at home with the Lord, 2 Corinthians 5:8.

For a Christian "to die is gain" Philippians 1:21. Therefore they need not be so tied to this earth that they perform futile operations just to extend life by a few more hours or days.

KARL BRANDT

"My underlying motive was the desire to help individuals who could not help themselves. Such considerations should not be regarded as inhuman. Nor did I feel it in any way to be unethical or immoral... I am convinced that if Hippocrates were alive today he would change the wording of his oath in which a doctor is forbidden to administer poison to an invalid even on demand.

I have a perfectly clear conscience about the part I played in the affair. I am perfectly conscious that when I said yes to euthanasia I did so with the greatest conviction, just as it is my conviction today that it is right."
Karl Brandt

Euthanasia as practiced by "Hitler's physician"

Here is the testimony of a doctor who was himself on trial for carrying out euthanasia.

These are the words of Karl Brandt, who was known as "Hitler's physician." He was the doctor in charge of the German euthanasia program during World War II. He presided over the deaths of millions of Jews, Slavs and so-called "defective" Germans. After the end of the war he was put on trial at Nuremberg in 1948 and hanged for his evil deeds.

BRITISH MEDICAL ASSOCIATION STATEMENT

"The evidence given in the trials of medical war criminals has shocked the medical profession and the world. These trials have shown that the doctors who were guilty of these crimes against humanity lacked both the moral and professional conscience that is to be expected of mem¹ ers of this honorable profession. They departed from the traditional medical ethic which maintains the value and sanctity of every individual human being. Whatever the causes such crimes must never be allowed to recur. Research in medicine as well as its practice must never be separated from eternal moral values. Doctors must be quick to point out to their fellow members of society the likely consequences of policies that degrade or deny fundamental human rights.

The profession must be vigilant to observe and to combat developments which might again ensnare its members and debase the high purpose of its ideals.

Although there have been many changes in medicine, the spirit of the Hippocratic Oath cannot change and must be reaffirmed by the profession. It enjoins the duty of caring, the greatest crime being cooperation in the destruction of life by murder, suicide and abortion."
British Medical Association Statement, 1947

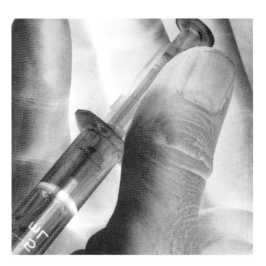

Helping people who could not help themselves

He said that his "underlying motive was the desire to help people who could not help themselves." If his testimony is taken at face value we conclude that he sincerely believed he was doing a favor to those people whose deaths he arranged.

Later testimony given at the Nuremberg Trials show that he was not alone in this perverse belief. But how could such apparently good intentions end in such unspeakable consequences?

"Merely a subtle shift in emphasis"

Dr Leo Alexander, a psychiatrist who worked with the Office of the Chief of Counsel for War Crimes at Nuremberg, sheds light on what he believed had happened in Germany before World War II which made Brandt's actions possible. The following extract by Dr Alexander is taken from the July 1949 edition of the *New England Medical Journal*.

"The beginnings at first were merely a subtle shift in emphasis in the basic attitude of the physicians. It started with the attitude, basic in the euthanasia movement that there is such a thing as a life not worthy to be lived. This attitude in its early stages concerned itself merely with severely and chronically sick. Gradually the sphere of those to be included in this category was enlarged to encompass the socially unproductive, the ideologically unwanted, the racially unwanted and finally all non-Germans."

In view of the current medical practice about euthanasia the British Medical Association's warning given in 1947, remains relevant.

The Dutch experience

A survey of Dutch physicians was taken in 1990 by the Remmelink Committee. They found that 1,030 patients were killed without their consent. Of these,

- 140 were fully mentally competent and
- 110 were only slightly mentally impaired.

The report also found that another 14,175 patients (1,701 of whom were mentally competent) were denied medical treatment without their consent and died.

Doctors in the United States and the Netherlands have found that though euthanasia was originally intended for exceptional cases, it has become an accepted way of dealing with serious or terminal illness.

60% of Dutch physicians do not report their cases of assisted suicide (even though reporting is required by law).

25% of Dutch physicians admit to ending patients' lives without their consent.

Holland and Belgium legalize euthanasia, 2001

Following the lead given in 2000 by Holland, in November 2001, the Belgium upper house passed the necessary legislation by 44 votes to 23 to legalize euthanasia. According to the provisions of the new law, patients wishing to end their lives must be over 18 and must make a specific request in writing. One month must then elapse before the "mercy killing" is administered.

"We've got used to it now"

One of the doctors who did one of the first euthanasia cases in Holland said: "Well, the first one we did, we agonized over, and it was absolutely dreadful. We were glad when it was all over. The second one was almost as difficult, but

PETER SINGER

"We can no longer base our ethics on the idea that human beings are a special form of creation, made in the image of God.

Once the religious mumbo-jumbo surrounding the term 'human' has been stripped away, we may continue to see normal members of our species as possessing greater qualities of rationality, self consciousness, communication and so on than members of any other species, but we will not regard as sacrosanct the life of every member of our species, no matter how limited its capacity for intelligent or even conscious life may be.

If we can put aside the obsolete and erroneous notion of the sanctity of all human life, we may start to look at human life as it really is, at the quality of human life that each human being has or can achieve."
Peter Singer, 'Sanctity of Life or Quality of Life?' Pediatrics, 1983, 72(1) pp.128-9.

not quite." Then he said, "We've got used to it now."

He implied that it was now easy. This sums up the whole situation. Once you go down that slippery slope, euthenasia becomes an easy thing for a doctor to perform on a routine and regular basis.

The Dutch Ministry of Justice

The Dutch Ministry of Justice commissioned the *Remmelink Report*, which revealed that in 2001 there were 2,300 cases of voluntary euthanasia and over 1,000 cases of involuntary euthanasia in Holland.

Dr Admiraal

A former President of the Dutch Society of Anaesthesiology, Dr Admiraal, now heads up one of the largest units for terminally ill patients in Holland. He calls himself his patients' friend. He assures them that he will give them an easy and painless death.

He has said, "I inject them with normal drugs used in anaesthesia and their suffering stops. This final act of terminal care has enriched my life as a doctor."

Holland

In Holland 3% of all deaths are directly caused by doctors.

If that same percentage applied in the United States, deaths caused by doctors would amount to 64,860 a year.

According to a poll conducted by the Dutch government, Dutch physicians now are performing two and a half times more involuntary euthanasia than voluntary.

Professor Spitzer believes that, "If this progression of events can occur in Holland, why couldn't such a progression of events occur in the US? Once physicians suddenly see there is this easy way out, once they see there is no necessity of moving through the unpleasantness of telling somebody that they have to die, then why shouldn't they work to make euthanasia mandatory?"

Euthanasia: "an economic necessity"

Some financiers are on record as saying that euthanasia is an economic necessity. The President of the European Bank for Reconstruction and Development, Jacques Attali, has stated, "As soon as he goes beyond 60-65 years of age man lives beyond his capacity to produce, and he costs society a lot of money. Euthanasia will be one of the essential instruments of our future societies."

Is the sanctity of all human life an obsolete notion?

Peter Singer is the influential Director of the Center for Human Bioethics in Melbourne, and editor of the *Bioethics Journal*. ["Bioethics" is concerned with the interface between ethics and modern medical technology as it affects the control of human life.] Singer set out his basic ideas in a leading American pediatric journal:

Voices against euthanasia
1. Walker Percy

Not everyone is in favor of the practice of euthanasia. The late award-winning novelist Walker Percy has said that the so-called "tenderness of euthanasia leads inevitably to the gas chamber, to

societies in which the scope for mercy killings swells to include not only the terminally ill, but those deemed socially useless as well."

2. The Ramsay Colloquium

The Ramsey Colloquium, a periodic gathering of prominent Jewish and Christian ethicists and thinkers, published a *Declaration on Euthanasia* to help fight the trend towards the growing toleration of the practice of assisted suicide. The *Declaration on Euthanasia* stated:

"Euthanasia is contrary to our faith as Jews and Christians, is based upon a grave moral error, does violence to our political tradition, and undermines the integrity of the medical profession.

In relating to the sick, the suffering, the incompetent, the disabled and the dying, we must learn again the wisdom that teaches us always to care and never to kill. Though it sometimes seems compassionate, killing is never a means of caring."

Lethal consequences

Ethicists are unanimous in predicting such a shift in values will extend the scope of cases in which euthanasia will be seen as legitimate. The former Surgeon General, C. Everett Koop has said:

"I am convinced that in the 1930s the German medical sentiment favoring euthanasia (even before Hitler came to power) made it easier for the Nazi government to move society along the slippery slope that led to the Holocaust."

5 *GLOBAL RELATIONSHIPS*

Introduction

When considering some of today's global problems we find ourselves wrestling with moral choices that have tested the minds of the greatest Christian thinkers over the past 2,000 years. Sometimes there are still no easy answers.

We know that we are meant to be salt and light, Matthew 5:13-16, in our society. So in addition to seeking to have our minds renewed by God's Spirit, Romans 12:2, we must never neglect the Christian way of life as it affects us personally. What would be the point of becoming the greatest Christian thinker of the day on topics such as ethics and morals, if one's personal walk with our Lord was in shreds?

Salt and light

Here are a few reminders about how we should strengthen our own spiritual walk with Jesus, as we seek to preserve all that is good in our society and give God's perspective on today's moral issues.

1. Do the right thing, no matter what

This means doing right, even when we feel that everyone else is doing wrong. See 1 Peter 3:20.

2. Do the right thing, even when you might have benefited materially from sin

- Recall what Moses gave up: Hebrews 11:24-26

- Remember how one young man put wealth before following Jesus: Matthew 19:22
- Resolve never to have the same epitaph as Demas. "Do your best to come to me quickly, for Demas, because he loved this world, deserted me." 2 Timothy 4:10.
- Renounce evil in any way that is applicable in your life: see Acts 19:19-20.

3. Do the right thing even when nobody else may know

Contrast the behavior of Joseph with Potiphar's wife, Genesis 39:7-20, with Achan's sin, Joshua 7:20-21, which he thought nobody would ever discover.

4. Do the right thing, even if it means being persecuted

Now few of us are going to be martyred for sticking to Christian principles. But this does not mean that we may not be laughed at, mocked and cold-shouldered.

Jesus warned his followers to expect persecution, see Matthew 5:10-12. So perhaps if we never suffer in any way for being a follower of Jesus we should ask ourselves a few questions.

Paul specifically told Timothy what the result would be if he led a godly life, see 2 Timothy 3:12.

Multi-racialism: should we pretend to be color-blind?

Martin Luther King's dream

"I have a dream that my four little children will one day live in a nation where they will not be judged by the color of their skin but by the content of their character.

I have a dream that one day in Alabama…little black boys and black girls will be able to join hands with little white boys and white girls as sisters and brothers." *Extract from Martin Luther King's 28 August, 1963, speech in Washington DC, at the head of a 250,000 strong march*

Revelation's vision

Martin Luther King worked tirelessly for non-discrimination, as well as for non-violence. In heaven we know that there will be no racial discrimination.

"After this I looked and there before me was a great multitude that no one could count, from every nation, tribe, people and language, standing before the throne and in front of the Lamb." *Revelation 7:9*

Racism has not been eradicated

The extreme racist views of Hitler are not dead.

- "Intermarriage [between people of different races] is a sin against the will of the Eternal Creator." *Adolf Hitler*
- "The Americans ought to be ashamed of themselves for letting their medals be won by Negroes." *Adolf Hitler*

- "All who are not of good race in this world are chaff." *Adolf Hitler*

Multi-racism and the God of creation

We know that God created our universe, Genesis 1:1. Paul told the Athenian philosophers, "From one man he [God] made every nation of men, that they should inhabit the whole earth" Acts 17:26.

God is the God of all human beings. This should determine our attitude to everyone one God's earth.

Multi-racism and the God of history

Paul continues in Acts 17:26, "and he [God] determined the times set for them and the exact places where they should live." Paul alludes to the time when God told humankind to multiply and fill the earth. "When the Most High gave the nations their inheritance, when he divided all mankind, he set up boundaries for the peoples according to the number of the sons of Israel" Deuteronomy 32:8. God's people dispersed with God's blessing and this was bound to lead to distinctive cultures developing.

Heaven will be enriched by human cultures, as "the kings of the earth will bring their splendor into it," and "the glory and honor of the nations will be brought into it" Revelation 21:24, 26. If that is going to be the case in heaven, we should be enriched by different human cultures on earth. We certainly should not be against this!

Race in the Bible

The primary teaching in the Bible about race concerns the unity of the human race.

- This is seen in creation: Genesis 1:28; 5:1
- This is also seen in the scope of salvation: Genesis 12:3; Matthew 28:19; Colossians 3:11; Revelation 5:9

The Samaritans in the New Testament

The Samaritans were hated by Jews because of their religion and also because of their race. Jesus went out of his way to show his love for Samaritans.

It is no accident that John 4 records Jesus' long conversation with the woman from Samaria.

Jesus deliberately chose the despised, half-caste, foreigner, a Samaritan, to be the hero of his parable which we know today as the Good Samaritan, Luke 10:25-37.

Paul

The apostle Paul himself was the product of three cultures. By background, family tree and upbringing he was a Jew, a "Hebrew of the Hebrews." But he had absorbed the Greek language and its concepts and he was proud of being a Roman citizen.

Paul stressed to Christians that they

NON-VIOLENT APPROACHES TO RACISM

Impractical and immoral

"Violence as a way of achieving racial justice is both impractical and immoral.

It is impractical because it is a descending spiral ending in destruction for all.

The old law of an eye for an eye leaves everyone blind.

It is immoral because it seeks to humiliate the opponent rather than win his understanding; it seeks to annihilate rather than convert. Violence is immoral because it thrives on hatred rather than love. It destroys community and makes brotherhood impossible. It leaves society in monologue rather than dialogue.

Violence ends by defeating itself. It creates bitterness in the survivors and brutality in the destroyers."
Martin Luther King Jr.

An article of faith

"Non-violence is the article of faith."
Mahatma Gandhi

An active force

"In my opinion non-violence is not passivity in any shape or form. Non-violence as I understand it is the most active force in the world."
Mahatma Gandhi

Preach and pray

"Preach and pray, but do not fight."
Martin Luther, advising those reformers who might have become revolutionaries

---

now belonged to God's family and that this superceded all human barriers and distinctions which they had previously belonged to.

"You are all sons of God through faith in Christ Jesus, for all of you who were baptized into Christ have clothed yourselves with Christ. There is neither Jew nor Greek, slave nor free, male nor female, for you are all one in Christ Jesus." See Colossians 3:11

The piano

"God knew what he was doing when he made me black. On a piano you cannot play a good tune using only the white notes: you must use the black and white notes together. God wants to play tunes with both his white notes and his black ones."
Dr Aggrey of Ghana

Am I prejudiced?

- Of course, prejudices extend beyond the color of someone's skin or hair style!
- Do I judge people according to their wealth?
- Do I judge people according to where they were born?
- Do I judge people according to who their parents were?
- Do I judge people according to their job?
- Do I judge people according to their skin-color?
- Do I judge people according to their accent?
- Do I judge people according to their age?
- Do I judge people according to what I can get out of them?
- Do I judge people according to their friends?
- Do I judge people according to their attitude towards me?
- Do I judge people according to their political beliefs?
- Do I judge people according to their social class?
- Am I against marriages between people of different races/nationality/skin-color?
- Would I let my daughter marry a white/black man?

IS RACIAL PREJUDICE BEING DEFEATED IN AMERICA?

1. Ask Martin Luther King

In December 1964 Martin Luther King received the Nobel Peace Prize, presented by King Olav of Norway, in recognition of his tireless campaign against oppression and prejudice.

In 1968 black dustmen had been on strike in Memphis for a week, and Martin Luther King went there to orchestrate a massive non-violent protest. Dr King was being put under pressure from some other black leaders like Stokely Carmichael because of his avowedly non-violent approach to gaining simple justice for American blacks.

He also referred to the numerous threats of violence he had received, some threatening his life. He said quite openly that he had been warned not to go to Memphis if he wanted to stay alive. He ended his last recorded public speech with these words:

"And then I got into Memphis and some began to talk about the threats of what would happen to me from some of our sick white brothers. But I don't know what will happen now. We've got some difficult days ahead. But it really doesn't matter now. Because I've been to the mountain-top and I don't mind. Like anybody, I would like to live a long life; longevity has its place, but I'm not concerned about that now. I just want to do God's will, and he's allowed me to go up to the mountain."

The following morning Dr King was taking a short break on the balcony of the Lorraine Motel, where he was engaged in a conference. As he turned to return to his room, the assassin's bullet rang out, making a direct, deadly hit on Dr King's face. He never recovered consciousness.

On hearing the news, President Johnson said to the American nation on TV: "I ask every citizen to reject the blind violence that has struck Dr King."

On Dr King's tombstone are inscribed the words:
FREE AT LAST,
FREE AT LAST,
THANK GOD ALMIGHTY
I'M FREE AT LAST.

2. Ask Tiger Woods

When Tiger Woods won the 1997 US Masters Golf tournament at the Augusta National Club he broke many records.

Aged 21, he became the youngest person to win the title.

His 12-stroke lead was a record.

He also set a course record with his 18 under par over the four rounds.

He was the first black person to win any of the four major US golf competitions (Woods is part African-American, part Cherokee, part Thai, and part Chinese."

In 1991 the Augusta National Golf Club had no ethnic minority members.

Medical research: should we do it just because we now can do it? Cloning

Dr Seed

The Chicago physicist, Dr Seed says that cloning will enable humanity to become "closer to God."

In February 2001 a bill to ban human cloning was shelved in the Senate due to differences over what constitutes a human life entitled to legal protection.

But under the 1990 Human Fertilization and Embryology Act it is legal in Britain to experiment on and destroy embryos up to 14 days old.

What cloning could do

Cloning by nuclear replacement could reprogram embryonic cells to produce tissues or organs genetically identical to those of existing human beings, thus avoiding rejection after transplantation.

DOLLY

In 1997 Dolly the lamb arrived. Dolly was a genetically identical copy of an adult sheep – a clone. She was the first mammal to be cloned.

In 1996, Ian Wilmut using an udder cell produced a new sheep. The result was Dolly. Dolly is a copy, a clone of the sheep whose udder cell was used.

But Dolly the sheep was only produced after 277 unsuccessful attempts.

Definition

A clone, from the Greek word *klon*, is an individual, plant, animal or human being, derived by asexual reproduction from another organism that has the identical hereditary components.

Individuals could derive from the same cell (identical twins), or the clone could originate from the cell of another individual.

Are humans allowed to clone?

Are we allowed to use the cloning technique?

We know that God appointed us to rule over all other creatures, Genesis 1:28. Many Christians feel that this gives biblical warrant for cloning in general, that is, cloning any animals but humans.

SO WHAT'S THE PROBLEM ABOUT CLONING?

People fear that we are moving into an area of technology that seems out of control. A German scientist, Stockinger, put it like this in *Der Spiegel*, in 1997: "Biologists and doctors anywhere in the world could hit upon the idea of generating genetically identical copies of geniuses, top-class athletes, artists or movie stars. The person off the shelf, or '*Homo xerox*' would no longer be mere fiction. Even Hitlers and Stalins could be produced in the labs of bio-modelers if only one usable cell of theirs could be found."

A dividing line between humans and animals

Today many non-Christian scientists see no difference between the animal kingdom and humans, in the sense that they feel at liberty to apply the same ethical standards to them.

This is not the case with the Bible's teaching. For the Bible draws a clear line between animals and humans.

What is the big difference between humans and animals?

- Humans were created in God's image. Animals were not created in God's image, Genesis 1:27.
- Human existence extends beyond physical death, while animal existence does not, Luke 16:19-31, Philippians 1:23.
- God allowed humans to kill animals, Genesis 9:2-3, but not fellow-humans, Exodus 20:13.
- God gave humans the responsibility to have dominion over the animal kingdom, Genesis 1:26, but were not told to have dominion over other humans
- This last point has a bearing on cloning. For humans were never meant to dominate other humans, or to manipulate them, which is just what cloning a human being would mean. God intended humans to have fathers and mothers, but a human clone could never have two parents.

A Christian perspective

All human beings are of infinite worth in God's sight, regardless of age or disability. Diversity among human beings is part of God's design. God has made us stewards of his creation. This validates scientific enquiry and application of scientific discoveries for the benefit of humankind. Where would we be today without anesthetics? However, the end never justifies the means. This is particularly relevant when it comes to destroying existing human life. This applies to embryonic life.

Conclusion

Christians are completely opposed to human cloning for the following reasons:

- Cloning can treat human beings as consumer items cutting across the diversity
  that the Creator has designed.
- Research that is involved in cloning often uses human embryos.
- Cloning by nuclear replacement is asexual reproduction (the clone has only one parent contributing DNA). This violates the principles of Genesis 2:24 and also means that the clone has only one genetic parent.
- Cloning of whole human beings could never be justified. However, the cloning of certain tissues (e.g. to produce skin grafts) may well be an acceptable application of the technology.

Positives

If cloning can be achieved without the use of human embryos it may open up exciting therapeutic possibilities in research into:

- ageing
- cancer
- infertility
- miscarriage
- congenital diseases.

Human rights

Solzhenistsyn

In his Nobel Prize speech in 1970, Solzhenistsyn said: "There is no internal affairs left on this globe of ours. Mankind can be saved only if everybody takes an interest in everybody else's affairs."

Human dignity

Christians have a very high view of humankind. From the first book in the Bible Christians assert something very important about:

Our relationship to God

"God created man in his own image," Genesis 1:27. The divine image in humans enables us to worship God and to relate to God.

BASIC HUMAN RIGHT NUMBER ONE

It should be a basic human right in every country for Christians to be free to worship, evangelize and teach the Christian faith.

Where this is not the case we need to join hands with those who campaign to bring about change.

Our relationship to each other

"The Lord God said, 'It is not good for a man to be alone. I will make a helper suitable for him'" Genesis 2:18. God made us social beings.

God created us "male and female" Genesis 1:27, with the order to have children and populate the world.

"God blessed them and said to them, 'Be fruitful and increase in number; fill the earth...'"

BASIC HUMAN RIGHT NUMBER TWO

It should be a basic human right in every country for everyone to be free to marry and have children, to meet together (peacefully), and to receive respect, regardless of sex, age, race or job.

Our relationship with the earth

"...subdue it [the earth]. Rule over the fish of the sea and the birds of the air and over every living creature that moves on the ground" Genesis 1:28. The dominion humans have over the earth and its animals brings with it great responsibilities.

BASIC HUMAN RIGHT NUMBER THREE

It should be a basic human right in every country that people have the right to work and to rest, the right to food, water and shelter and medical care. We are to share not horde and over-indulge ourselves with the earth's resources.

Human rights and faith in God

A former Archbishop of Canterbury, William Temple, once said:

"There can be no Rights of Man except on the basis of faith in God. But if God is real, and all men and women are created by him, that is the true worth of every one of them. *My worth is what I am worth to God;* and that is a marvelous great deal, for Christ died for me. Thus, incidentally, what gives to each of us his highest worth gives the same worth to everyone; in all that matters most we are all equal."

God has no favorites

"For the Lord your God is God of gods and Lord of lords, the great God, mighty and awesome, who shows no partiality and accepts no bribes" *Deuteronomy 10:17.* As God was just, so Israel's judges were meant to be just, see Deuteronomy 16:18, 19.

This is the basis for Christians saying that justice is a basic human right. Where such human rights are denied, or where humans are abused sexually or through torture or in any other way it should so outrage Christians that we act to fight against such evils.

"Torture kills the human in the torturer and crushes the personality of the one tortured." *Dr Emilio Castro*

What can I do?

1. Consider joining an organization that campaigns for human rights, such as Amnesty International.
2. Write letters. Governments are still sensitive to international pressure, and they also do not like receiving letters complaining about people being abused in their own country.
3. Be a good example. Christian fellowships, are meant to be a sign of God's rule and way of life. The hallmark of Christian churches should be an absence of favoritism, abuse and discrimination, and an abundance of self-renunciation and affirmation of mutual responsibility and care for each other.

Poverty and global inequalities

A basic human right

Christians believe that it is a basic human right that no one in the world should go to sleep starving, freezing with cold through lack of clothing and bedding, and without a roof over their head.

Our global village

When we see pictures on TV of young children crying with their grossly extended stomachs, what do we do? Better still, what should we do?

Change channels. Some people can't bear to watch such human suffering. This does not mean necessarily that they are uncaring, it could mean that they just can't cope with such human sadness.

Phone a relief agency and make a donation with a credit card.

Watch the TV, making sure it has no effect on them whatsoever.

Decide to support a relief agency on a monthly basis. Some Christians have scruples about supporting a relief agency that is not run by Christians. But as there are so many Christian relief agencies to choose from today we can no longer use this as a way of escape.

Say, "How terrible." It makes us remember that:

- One in four of the world's people today lives in a state of absolute poverty.
- 35,000 children die every day because they are poor.

- 130 million children do not attend primary school, 70%of them girls.
- 1.3 billion people have no safe water or sanitation.

Be positive

Most of us throw up our hands in horror or desperation when confronted with a cameo of our suffering world. But we feel that the problem is so huge that there is nothing that can be done about it, and definitely, our little contribution would make no difference to the scale of the problem.

But aid agencies now take pains to point out to us that: Already in the "developing countries" of Africa, Asia and Latin America progress has been made over the past few decades:

- death rates of children have been cut by half since 1960;
- life expectancy has gone up from 41 to 62 years;
- twice as many people now have safe water to drink.

The elimination of poverty is affordable and achievable – if individuals and communities want and demand it.

Education

"Educating young people to became Global Citizens will ensure that they are able to work for a more secure and sustainable future.

Young people today are not passive or complacent.

They are concerned about:

- the destruction of the rainforests,
- that many people in the world go hungry,
- that conflict affects the lives of people in both North and South.

By incorporating the principles of Global Citizenship into education, we can enable young people to develop these concerns, challenge poverty and injustice, and take real effective action for change." *Oxfam Report*

Change can come

Our world with its terrible inequalities, with the rich north getting richer and richer while the poor south becomes poorer and poorer, can be changed. This change depends on our:

- values and attitudes
- sense of identity and self-esteem
- empathy
- commitment to social justice and equity
- value and respect for diversity
- concern for the environment and commitment to sustainable development.
- belief that people can make a difference.

Fair trade

There are many products like coffee and tea, which are now sold in our supermarkets and that guarantee that the people who have produced them have been given reasonable wages. We should support such wholesome enterprises.

Third world debt

Many of the poorest countries in the world spend such a high proportion of their income servicing their debts that their economies will never recover, and their desire for basic education and medical care will never come about.

Such debts should be written off and these countries should be relieved of these impossible burdens.

Conclusion

The Bible is on the side of the poor and the disadvantaged. The rich western countries need to apply the principles of mercy and justice to the desperately poor nations of our one world. Our actions should be based on the words of Micah 6:8: "He has showed you, O man, what is good. And what does the Lord require of you? To act justly and to love mercy and to walk humbly with your God."

Environment: should all Christians be green?

Looking after the environment

PIONEERS
"We should be pioneers in the care of mankind."
Klaus Bockmühl

REJECTION OF GOD
"The destruction of the world around us is a reflection of not being 'God centered' as human beings. Christ, as both God and man, is our center, our truth and our life. The pollution and defilement we encounter exists through ignorance or rejection of God."
Tod Connor

CHILDREN OF OUR LANDSCAPE
"We are children of our landscape."
Lawrence Durrell

A CRISIS IN HUMAN BEINGS
"What we call the environmental crisis is not merely a crisis in the natural environment of human beings. It is nothing less than a crisis in human beings themselves."
Jurgen Moltman

MONEY CANNOT BE EATEN
"Only after the last tree has been cut down,
Only after the last river has been poisoned,
Only after the last fish has been caught,
Only then will you find that money cannot be eaten."
Cree Indian
Proverb

LOVE AND RESPECT
"Loving the Lover who has made the world, I should have respect for the thing He has made."
Francis Schaeffer

FOSSIL FUELS
"If we squander our fossil fuels, we threaten civilization, but if we squander the capital represented by living nature around us, we threaten life itself."
E. F. Schumacher

DEPENDENCE AND DOMINION
"Our intermediate position is between God and nature, between the Creator

and the rest of his creation. We combine dependence on God with dominion over the earth."
John Stott

GREENERY
"It is forbidden to live in a city that does not have greenery."
Jerusalem Talmud, Kiddushin 12:12

The earth belongs to God
"The earth is the Lord's, and everything in it." *Psalm 24:1*

God created the universe. The earth belongs to God.

God is the Creator
"In the beginning God created the heavens and the earth." *Genesis 1:1*

The fact that God created the world means that he owns it. Humans should not really claim ownership over anything. Everything we have comes from God who created it all. We certainly have no right to exploit God's creation.

We are stewards, caring for God's world
"The highest heavens belong to the Lord; but the earth he has given to man." *Psalm 115:16*

In Genesis 1:26 we read: "Let them have dominion over the earth." God has given the responsibility of looking after his world to humans: "...and subdue it" Genesis 1:28.

The one thing a steward has to do is

to be found faithful in looking after all that is put in his charge. In that sense Christians ought to be conscientious about caring for God's world and all his creatures, and avoid waste and unnecessary depletion of earth's resources. In that sense all Christians should be green and friends of the earth and our environment.

In Matthew 6:28-29, God tells us that he clothes the lilies of the field. Furthermore, not even a sparrow falls without God's knowledge and permission, Matthew 10:29. Since God is that concerned about his creatures, we, acting as his stewards, must be similarly concerned.

An environmental ethic
We need to develop a Christian environmental ethic based on the Bible, and we need to practice it.

- The earth must be ruled sensitively.
- We should reject needless exploitation of the creation for selfish gain.
- We look forward to God's new heaven and a new earth in which righteousness lives: Revelation 21:1 – 22:5; Isaiah 55:1 – 56:2.

Waste matters
Question:
What practical steps can I take to help the environment?
Answer:
If everyone disposed of their own family's waste in an environmentally

positive way landfill waste sites would take twice as long to fill.

We can all sort our own waste into:

- paper
- cardboard
- plastic
- used tins
- glass and bottles
- compost

and deposit it in the appropriate place.

The human factor

Faced with global ecological pollution, most of us shrug our shoulders and mumble to ourselves, "If only somebody would do something about it."

The problem often has more to do with the will of humans than with our lack of knowledge about environmentally friendly methods to keep our planet clean. In his book, *The Seventh Enemy*, Ronald Higgins lists as his first six "enemies:"

- the population explosion
- the food crisis
- the scarcity of resources
- environmental degradation
- nuclear abuse
- scientific technology.

The seventh "enemy" is men and women. The sub-title to Higgins' book is "The Human Factor in the Global Crisis."

How we react to the constant onslaught on our environment can influence the decision-makers and those who wield power in industry and business.

Energy matters

Question:

How can I help to keep greenhouse gases to a minimum?

Answers:

1. Your car

Most Americans do not naturally warm to the most obvious answer to this question. To choose a car that is more environmentally friendly and less gas-guzzling would drastically reduce the consumption of the world's limited supply of oil.

2. Your electricity bill

Most of us need to change the habits of a lifetime. So when we buy an electric bulb, we may know that energy-saving, 5-7 year lasting bulbs, are much better for the environment and are cheaper in the long run. But most of still just buy ordinary lightbulbs.

When buying a new fridge or freezer or washing machine we now can opt for one that uses less electricity and has economy washes.

In the supermarket

None of us likes the thought of chickens being raised or fattened up in cages or tiny compartments, yet relatively few of us opt for free-range eggs and free-range chickens.

Many farmers use cruel methods to raise calves and pigs. But we have the option not to buy such products and only purchase meat that comes from farmers who use animal- friendly methods.

It all boils down to economics. The supermarkets demand certain cuts of meat to be produced at rock-bottom prices. So the farmers comply with such demands. At present meat produced by farmers who use animal-friendly methods is much more expensive than meat that is produced in ways that are now called traditional mass-produced techniques. But the more we buy meat produced in an animal-friendly way the more it will come down in price.

In the garden
Most of us think nothing of spraying our flowers to attack greenfly. But such pesticides are far from being environmentally friendly. Then there are the weeds. Once again we buy chemicals and apply them without a second thought. But organic substitutes are now widely available and if we always use them we would be doing our little bit to keep our planet healthy.

What about large corporations?
It often appears that we, as individuals, will never have any impact on the activities of global organizations and their lack of environmentally friendly policies.

It seems that hardly a month goes by without some report being issued about big business causing pollution.

Disney park blamed for pollution
The construction of a new Disney theme park in Hong Kong has been condemned as an environmental disaster following evidence that 7,000,000 fish have died as a result of dredging work in the waters around one site.

Fishermen – whose livelihoods have been ruined – say that the sea has become so thick with mud that fish are unable to breathe. The habitat of the rare Chinese white dolphin is also under threat.

What can we do?
There are a number of organizations that monitor global pollution and protest about it. There are also a number of organizations that specialize in campaigning for the preservation of endangered animal species around the world. Although such organizations may not be specifically Christian the good they do would be enhanced if more Christians supported them.

Warfare: is there such a thing as a just war?

Seemingly conflicting scriptures

TOTAL DESTRUCTION

"When the Lord your God has delivered them [the enemy] over to you and you have defeated them, then you must destroy them totally. Make no treaty with them, and show them no mercy."
Deuteronomy 7:2

TURN THE OTHER CHEEK

"But I tell you, do not resist him who is evil. If someone strikes you on the right cheek, turn to him the other also."
Matthew 5:39

LOVE YOUR ENEMIES

"But I say to you who hear, love your enemies, do good to those who hate you."
Luke 6:27

THE SWORD

"But if you do wrong, be afraid; for it [the governing authority] does not bear the sword for nothing. It is God's servant, an angel of wrath to bring punishment on the wrongdoer."
Romans 13:4

Contradictory scriptures?

How can those who believe in the "just war" be comfortable with Bible verses that seem to be against war?

Such apparent inconsistencies may be resolved by reading the verses in their context.

The "turn the other cheek" group of scriptures is not in the context of national defense. As Christians are citizens of nation states in addition to being members of the Christian church, most Christians have interpreted these words of Jesus in a way that allows them to fight for their country.

However, the context of Romans 13 is to do with the actions of a government. In this case the governing authorities, Romans 13:1, do have the right to bear the sword, Romans 13:4, so long as it done in order to protect the life and welfare of its citizens. "The authorities that exist have been created by God" Romans 13:1

The context of Deuteronomy 7:2 is that of a theocracy, in which God directly rules the nation. Its command was given to the Israelites so that they could remove the pagan Canaanites from the land God had given to them. This is hardly the situation in any country today.

DIFFERENT VIEWS ABOUT WAR

War and peace
"We make war that we may live in peace." *Aristotle*

A wrong deed
"To bomb cities as cities, deliberately to attack civilians, quite irrespective of whether or not they are actively contributing to the war effort, is a wrong deed, whether done by the Nazis or by ourselves." *George Bell*

Theft
"Every gun that is made, every warship launched, every rocket fired signifies in the final sense, a theft from those who hunger and are not fed, those who are cold and are not clothed. This world [traffic or trade?] in arms is not spending money alone. It is spending the sweat of its laborers, the genius of its scientists, the hopes of its children. This is not a way of life at all in any true sense. Under the clouds of war, it is humanity hanging on a cross of iron." *Dwight Eisenhower, April 16, 1953*

A good war?
"There never was a good war or a bad peace." *Benjamin Franklin*

Iniquity
"For the Christian who believes in Jesus and his Gospel, war is an iniquity and a contradiction." *Pope John XXIII*

An end to war
"Mankind must put an end to war, or war will put an end to mankind." *John F. Kennedy*

Prophetic
"The past is prophetic in that it asserts loudly that wars are poor chisels for carving out peaceful tomorrows." *Martin Luther King*

It will never go off
"The atomic bomb is the biggest fool thing we have ever done. The bomb will never go off. I speak as an expert in explosives." *Admiral William Leahy, US chief of staff*

The lesser evil
"War is evil, but it is often the lesser evil." *George Orwell*

Unparalleled catastrophe
"The unleashed power of the atom has changed everything save our modes of thinking; and thus we are drifting towards unparalleled catastrophe. A new type of thinking is essential if mankind is to survive." *Albert Einstein*

The just war
"In order for a war to be just, three things are necessary. First, the authority of the sovereign...Secondly, a just cause...Thirdly...a rightful intention." *Thomas Aquinas*

Three views
Broadly speaking there are three views
which Christians have, and do hold
about war:

1. Total pacifism
2. Relative pacifism, sometimes
   called nuclear pacifism
3. The just war theory

1. The total Christian pacifist
Some Christians take the view that all
war is evil and that no Christians should
take up arms in the defense of his/her
country.

The Christian pacifist is influenced by
the texts that say, "turn the other cheek,"
and "love your enemy." Some Christian
pacifists believe that their personal
convictions should be embraced by the
nation's government, so that the nation
itself does not involve itself in any way
in military activities.

Hating and loving
The Christian pacifist says:

- to hate those who love us is the
  devil's way;
- to love those who love us and hate
  those who hate us is the way of the
  world;
- to love those who hate us is the
  way of Jesus. See Matthew 5:38-48;
  Luke 6:27-36.

The example of Jesus
Jesus was innocent, and yet he suffered
terribly.

"He was led like a lamb to the
slaughter, and as a sheep before her
shearers is silent, so he did not open
his mouth." *Isaiah 53:7*

The pacifists conclude that the
teaching and the example of Jesus
indicate that the way forward for us is
by means of non-violence and non-
resistance.

Pacifists today
In the sixteenth century Anabaptist
groups were pacifist.

Today, groups such as Quakers,
Mennonites, United Brethren, sometimes
referred to as the "Peace Churches", as
well as some historic Reformation
churches support the pacifist view.

Pacifism
"The Spirit of Christ, which leads us
into all Truth, will never move us to
fight and war against any man with
outward weapons, neither for the
kingdom of Christ, nor for the kingdom
of this world." *Quaker Declaration, 1660*

Non-violence
"This house will in no circumstances
fight for its King and country."
*Motion passed at the Oxford Union, Oxford
University, 9 February 1933*

2. The just war
A second Christian approach to war may
be summed up by what is called "the
just war theory." The idea of the just war
theory pre-dates Christianity. But it was
Christianized by Augustine in the fourth

century, systematized by Thomas Aquinas in the thirteenth century,

developed by Francisco de Vitoria in the sixteenth century, and endorsed by a majority of the Reformers. Today it is held by most Roman Catholics and Protestants.

Seven conditions

The "just war" theory has sometimes been formulated under the following seven headings, which summarize the conditions which much exist before any war falls into the category of being a "just war."

- A formal declaration of war
- Last resort
- Just cause
- Right intention
- Proportionate means
- Noncombatant immunity
- Reasonable expectation.

Three criteria

These seven conditions may also be summarized under the following three headings:

1. For a war to be a "just" war its cause must be righteous.
2. For a war to be a "just" war its means must be controlled.
3. For a war to be a "just" war its outcome must be predictable.

Its causes must be righteous

- A "just" war must be a defensive war, not an aggressive war.

- A "just" war must have justice as its aim.
- A "just" war only takes place as a last resort, after all attempts at negotiation have been exhausted.
- A "just" war cannot take place if it is launched out of hatred revenge.

Its means must be controlled

- A "just" war excludes unnecessary violence.
- A "just" war is "proportionate" in that it is the lesser of two evils and the violence inflicted is proportionately less than that which it is intended to remedy.
- A "just" war is "discriminate" in the sense that it is directed against military targets and never deliberately aims to kill civilians.

Its outcome must be predictable

- A "just" war will only be engaged in after it has been calculated that there is a prospect for victory, which will achieve the just cause for which the war was started.

Is a "just" war biblical?

The key passages of Scripture here are Romans 12:17-21 and Romans 13:1-7. Christians, as members of God's community are all private individuals but may also be state officials.

As private individuals

As private individuals they should never repay evil for evil or seek revenge but should bless their persecutors, Romans 12:14, serve their enemies, Romans 12:20, and try to overcome evil with good, Romans 12:21.

As state officials

As state officials we may be God's agents in seeking that evildoers are punished. One way that God punishes evildoers is through the state. In that sense a state may be "an agent of wrath to bring punishment on the wrongdoer" Romans 13:4.

"So the development of the "just war" theory represented a systematic attempt to interpret acts of war by analogy with acts of civil government, and so to see them as belonging to the context of the administration of justice and as subject to the restraining standards of executive justice." *Oliver O'Donovan*

3. Relative or nuclear pacifism
A greatly increased capacity

All bombs dropped in World War II were the equivalent of 3 megatons of TNT.

Today, there are the equivalent of more than 18,000 megatons of TNT stockpiled in nuclear arsenals across the world.

It would only take 300 megatons to destroy all of the world's large and medium size cities.

Our nuclear age

Never before has so much destructive power been in the hands of sinful people. In addition to nuclear bombs other weapons of mass destruction, capable of inflicting unspeakable chemical and bacterial horrors, are now available to an increasing number of nations. Also, since 11 September 2001, the specter of these evil weapons falling into the hands of terrorists has been greatly heightened.

Because present-day weapons can inflict such sudden and devastating attacks, many "just war" advocates now think that preventative actions are compatible with the "just war" theory.

Now that we live in the era of nuclear weapons a new dimension has been added to all discussion about war. The possession of the "ABC" weapons (Atomic, Biological and Chemical) by some countries adds to this new dimension in all debates about war.

Non-resistance

Some Christians are willing to allow their government to go to war, since God has given human governments the right to govern themselves, Genesis 9:1-17. However, in such a situation, they themselves would only take part in was as non-combatants. They do not think it right for Christians to bear arms.

Their position differs from the pacifist view which will have no contact whatsoever with the military, as they are actually willing to work in civilian companies with military contracts as long as they can maintain a "make the bullet but not fire it" status.

Shedding innocent blood

The "shedding of innocent blood" is seen as a great evil in the Old Testament. As human life is made in the image of God it is sacrosanct.

"Whoever sheds the blood of man, by man shall his blood be shed, for in the image of God has God made man" Genesis 9:6. This means that the blood-shedding of murder deserves the blood-shedding of capital punishment. For in capital punishment it is the blood of the guilty that is shed. In all other cases the sin of "shedding innocent blood" has been committed.

It is this principle of the "shedding of innocent blood" that needs to be addressed in our attitude to war, especially as we now live in the age of atomic, biological and chemical weapons.

Atomic, biological and chemical weapons

The existence of atomic, biological and chemical weapons, especially nuclear weapons, which destroy on such a massive scale, challenges the relevance of the "just war" theory. Nuclear weapons can hardly be described as proportionate or discriminate or controlled. When a nuclear bomb is dropped a great deal of innocent blood is shed. It is clear that the indiscriminate use of atomic, biological and chemical weapons can never be justified. For many Christians a nuclear war could never be a just war.

"The New Abolitionist Covenant"

An ecumenical group (with strong evangelical participation) met in the United States in 1980 and drew a parallel between the nineteenth-century movement to abolish slavery and the need now for a movement to abolish nuclear weapons. "The New Abolitionist Covenant" states that: "Unlimited in their violence, indiscriminate in their victims, uncontrollable in their devastation, nuclear weapons have brought humanity to an historical crossroads. More than at any previous time in history, the alternatives are peace or destruction. In nuclear war there are no winners."

Questions raised by "The New Abolitionist Covenant"

There are a number of tough questions which nuclear pacifists have to answer. Because some Christians think that these questions cannot be answered satisfactorily there is no universal Christian consensus on being a nuclear pacifist.

1. Is the distinction between combatants and non-combatants obsolete?

The argument is that nuclear war is total war and there are no longer any non-combatants. Also, since the whole nation pays tax the responsibility for the manufacture of nuclear weapons can be said to extend to the whole nation. In that sense, runs the argument, everybody is a combatant.

Against this argument it has been

pointed out that elderly people and children would be killed in nuclear war and the killing of such non-combatants amounts to "killing innocent blood."

2. Not all nuclear weapons are indiscriminate

While this is true in theory the risk of escalation is so great that the only way for us to live in safety is for the nuclear button never to be pressed.

3. If the use of nuclear weapons would be evil, must not their retention as a deterrent be declared equally evil?

This is the third question asked of nuclear pacifists.

So we have reached the following stage in the argument. If we agreed that the use of global-nuclear weapons, with indiscriminate destruction being inevitable, would be immoral, and if we agreed that the risk of escalation is too great to justify the use of global-nuclear weapons, does that mean that all Christians have to agree to unilateral nuclear disarmament?

The answer is "no." Not all nuclear pacifists are unilateralists. It is quite reasonable to draw the moral distinction between possession, threat and use.

It can be argued that if an action is immoral, then the active threat to perform it is immoral too.

But the possession of nuclear weapons can be seen as more a conditional warning than an aggressive threat.

As everyone knows, the intention

behind America and Britain possessing a nuclear capacity is not to encourage the use of nuclear weapons, but to deter their use.

Tentative conclusion about the nuclear pacifist conviction

The rather illogical position of the nuclear pacifist is that he/she would like to renounce the use of nuclear weapons, but retain their possession. "Retaining possession, renouncing use" is quite justifiable morally but appears to be practically self-defeating.

But nuclear pacifists do claim to be idealists. They believe that the use of nuclear weapons on a global scale is immoral.

But nuclear pacifists maintain that they cling to this ideal and at the same time face the realities of our evil and fallen world.

Faced by an aggressor who threatened nuclear war on the United States this is how a president of the United States might argue, if he was a nuclear pacifist:

"We believe that the use of weapons of indiscriminate destruction would be mindless and immoral. So we are determined not to use them. We also think that you do not want to use them either. But if you attack us, you are likely to provoke us to act in a way that is against both our reason and our conscience. Don't put us in that position."

War and violence

Violence

Faced with the threat of war and violence Christians need to pray and contribute to peacemaking in every way possible.

QUOTATIONS ON VIOLENCE

Justifiable homicide?

"We should do unto others as we would want them to do unto us. If I were an unborn fetus I would want others to use force to protect me, therefore using force against abortionists is justifiable homicide."
"Pro-Life" doctor-killer Paul Hill

The modern choice

"The modern choice is between non-violence and non-existence."
Martin Luther King

Meaningless chaos

"If you succumb to the temptation of using violence in the struggle, unborn generations will be the recipients of a long and dissolute night of bitterness, and your chief legacy to the future will be an endless reign of meaningless chaos." *Martin Luther King*

Quest for identity?

"Violence is an involuntary quest for identity."
Marshall McLuhan

Armed revolt?

"In 1559 a more sinister turn was taken in the evangelical affairs. The persecuted church began to think in terms of armed resistance, even of armed revolt. The ranks of evangelicals now contained a large number of nobles, unused to suffering wrongs as patiently as the middle classes who had hitherto predominated...Calvin was sounded as to his opinions on active revolt. He had already, in a letter to the church in Paris, made it clear that he was aware of the new situation brought about by the change in the composition of the church, and had spoken out strongly against the use of force: 'Let it be your care to attempt nothing that is not warranted by his Word...It would be better for us all to be ruined than that the gospel of God should be exposed to the reproach that it has armed men for sedition and tumult.'"
T. H. L. Parker

Links to violence

"Let us not forget that violence does not exist by itself and cannot do so; it is necessarily interwoven with lies. Violence finds its only refuge in falsehood, falsehood its only support in violence. Any man who has once acclaimed violence as his method must inexorably choose falsehood as his principle."
Alexander Solzhenitsyn

War among Christians

What causes war?

A better question is: Who causes war? The answer is: we do. Yes, this includes Christians. James is crystal clear in his teaching on this topic. And we must bear in mind that James was writing to Christians.

Fights and quarrels

"From whence come wars and fightings among you?" *KJV*

"What causes fights and quarrels among you? Don't they come from your desires that battle within you? You want something but don't get it. You kill and covet, but you cannot have what you want. You quarrel and fight. You do not have, because you do not ask God.

When you ask, you do not receive, because you ask with wrong motives, that you may spend what you get on your pleasures." *James 4:1-3*

Questions to ask

How do we contribute to putting nations/races/communities/families on a war footing against each other?

Does losing my temper matter? Or does this help to make war on a personal basis?

Jesus said, "Blessed are the peacemakers" Matthew 5:9. So in what ways can I be a peacemaker at home/work/college this week? Are my attempts at peacemaking rather half-hearted, or can I really say that I have done what Paul says in Romans 14:19: "Let us therefore make every effort to do what leads to peace"?

James speaks about not having what we want being the cause of fights and quarrels. How does this apply to my life?

In certain countries, notably Indian and USA, it is common practice for Christians to take each other to court. If

I have a just cause for doing this should I proceed? Read 1 Corinthians 6:1-6. Taking some to court has become a way of life. But it should not be so among Christians. Paul's conclusions about this matter are totally at odds with goes on today.

---

1. Defeated

"The very fact that you have lawsuits among you means you have been completely defeated already."
1 Corinthians 6:7

---

2. Give way

"Why not rather be wronged? Why not rather be cheated?"
1 Corinthians 6:7

---

3. You cheat and do wrong

"Instead, you yourselves cheat and do wrong, and you do this to your brothers."
1 Corinthians 6:7

Do I harbor a grudge against any fellow-Christian? If so, Jesus says, "be reconciled to your brother" before you next worship God, see Matthew 5:24.

But what if a Christian brother has harmed me? Again Jesus' teaching is as difficult to put into practice as it is easy to understand: "Forgive your brother from your heart," Matthew 18:35. Do I encourage members of my own family to forgive each other and set a good personal example in this?

Global

We may wonder what infighting among Christians has to do with global warfare. The two are inextricably linked. If families are always at each others' throats it is hardly surprising that the same happens on the world stage.

The one group of people who should be exemplary in this matter, showing a new, peaceful way of living, should be Christian individuals, Christian families and Christian fellowships.